LACAN
FOR BEGINNERS™

The unconscious is structured like a language

I always speak the truth. Not the whole truth, because there is no way to say it all

The Woman does not exist

There is no such thing as a sexual relationship

WRITERS AND READERS PUBLISHING, INC.
P.O. Box 461, Village Station
New York, NY 10014

Writers and Readers Limited
9 Cynthia Street
London N1 9JF
England
•

A Writers and Readers Documentary Comic Book
Copyright © 1997
ISBN # 0-86316-227-4 Trade
1 2 3 4 5 6 7 8 9 0

Manufactured in the United States of America

Beginners Documentary Comic Books are published by Writers and Readers Publishing, Inc. Its trademark, consisting of the words "For Beginners, Writers and Readers Documentary Comic Books" and the Writers and Readers logo, is registered in the U. S. Patent and Trademark Office and in other countries.

Writers and Readers—
publishing FOR BEGINNERS™ books
continuously since 1975:

1975: Cuba • 1976: Marx • 1977: Lenin • 1978: Nuclear Power • 1979: Einstein • Freud • 1980: Mao • Trotsky • 1981: Capitalism • 1982: Darwin • Economists • French Revolution • Marx's Kapital • French Revolution • Food • Ecology • 1983: DNA • Ireland • 1984: London • Peace • Medicine • Orwell • Reagan • Nicaragua • Black History • 1985: Marx Diary • 1986: Zen • Psychiatry • Reich • Socialism • Computers • Brecht • Elvis • 1988: Architecture • Sex • JFK • Virginia Woolf • 1990: Nietzsche • Plato • Malcolm X • Judaism • 1991: WW II • Erotica • African History • 1992:Philosophy • Rainforests • Malcolm X • Miles Davis • Islam • Pan Africanism • 1993: Psychiatry • Black Women • Arabs & Israel • Freud • 1994: Babies • Foucault • Heidegger • Hemingway • Classical Music • 1995: Jazz • Jewish Holocaust • Health Care • Domestic Violence • Sartre • United Nations • Black Holocaust • Black Panthers • Martial Arts • History of Clowns • 1996: Opera • Biology • Saussure • UNICEF • Kierkegaard • Addiction & Recovery • I Ching • Buddha • Derrida • Chomsky • McLuhan • Jung • 1997: Lacan • Shakespeare • Structuralism

---

ACKNOWLEDGEMENTS

Thank you very much: Auriol Drew, Dylan Evans, Naomi Gryn, Ruth and Herman Hepner, Judy and Arthur Hill, Katie Hunter, Jolyon Jenkins, Michelle Julien, Joanna Knatchbull, Valerie Mitchell, Adam Poole, Poppy, Oliver Rathbone, Susanna Simons, Michael, Robert and Sammy Slowe.

Thank you to the following who have given permission for photos and art work to be used:

• Laylani Susman for her own fine illustrations on pages 17, 46 and 47.

• ITPS Ltd for permission to use photos of J. Neumann page 117], K. Gödel [page 116] and a torus [page 148].

• The Moschino Spring-Summer 1996 Advertising Campaign for the wonderful dress on page 104.

CONTENTS

The ideas expressed in this book do not necessarily reflect those of the author

LACAN

FOR BEGINNERS™

WRITTEN BY PHILIP HILL
ILLUSTRATED BY DAVID LEACH

Writers and Readers

WHAT IS PSYCHOANALYSIS?

Lacan always claimed that he was developing and formalising ideas that Sigmund Freud had worked on in the period from 1893 to 1938. Freud founded a new discipline and treatment: psychoanalysis. Psychoanalysis has two closely related aspects: clinical work and academic work. Clinical work is carried out with patients who suffer from a wide range of problems, including phobias, obsessions, impotence, anxiety, and hallucinations. The psychoanalyst uses only words in his treatment, no electric shocks, no massage or medicine. Academic psychoanalysis aims to study mental life in general and includes studies of literature and the social sciences.

Psychoanalysis has many links with other disciplines. While a close study of Lacan's theories demands a study of logic, science, philoso-phy, literature and other disciplines, Lacan's ideas were inspired above all by the clinic, by his work and experience with his clients. His theories, which some claim are overly intellectual, are only attempts to make sense of what he witnessed in his clinic, working with clients.

Divisions and Factions in Psychoanalysis

Lacan has probably been the most important and influential psychoanalyst since Freud. Worldwide there are some 20,000 psychoanalysts, that is people who work broadly in the Freudian tradition (this excludes followers of Jung). Roughly speaking psychoanalysts are equally divided into two camps: those influenced by Lacan's work, and those more or less loyal to the ideas of Ego Psychology and the International Psycho-Analytic Association.

The 10,000 psychoanalysts working with Lacan's ideas are mostly in France, Spain, Italy and South America. The other 10,000 influenced by the International Psychoanalytic Association are dominant in England and North America, where Lacan's influence has been felt least.

What is the difference
between psychoanalysis and
psychotherapy?

Psychotherapy is any non-medical attempt to help people with psychological problems, and ranges from electroshock aversion therapy, to hypnosis, to a variety of talking cures. But psychoanalysis is unique; it always follows the ideas of Freud and places the highest value on working with speech and desire.

CHAPTER 1

WHO WAS LACAN?

He became a skinny but handsome intellectual and a dandy. He was exempted from military service because of his physique.

Lacan underwent medical and psychiatric training, a personal psychoanalysis and became a man of charisma,

Jacques Lacan was born to a middle class French Catholic family in 1901, seven years after Freud's work was first published. Lacan would usually have his nose in a book while other boys were playing football.

the lover of many women,

 and an atheist.

5

During the Nazi occupation of France Lacan heard that the Nazis held a file on his Jewish wife, so he visited their headquarters and demanded to see the file. He then left with the file and destroyed it, saving his wife.

Lacan's difficult lectures were attended by many leading psychoanalysts and intellectuals. There would often be lengthy silences, in between Lacan writing obscure symbols and formulae on a blackboard. Listeners were often baffled by his complicated word plays and enigmatic puns, and by his use of German, Hebrew, Chinese and Ancient Greek. Even French speakers attending his talks were not sure if he was speaking French or not. Now, more than fifteen years after his death, there is a cult following of Lacan, with some thirty different camps of bickering followers, each claiming loyalty to the master.

Most of Lacan's work was not published or otherwise written down; he simply spoke it at his weekly seminars and lectures.

But my `Ecrits' were published in my lifetime

Some of Lacan's tape-recorded talks have been published and translated, but much of his work remains unpublished or untranslated; it circulates only in 'samizdat' form, as unofficial transcripts of the seminars. Lacan scorned publication, pronouncing it as 'poubellication', from the French 'poubelle', for garbage can.

The clinical and theoretical innovations introduced by Lacan (such as his infamous clinical sessions of variable length that could last any time between five minutes and an hour, instead of the conventional fifty minutes) produced splits in the psychoanalytic movement, and finally led to his being expelled from the International Psychoanalytic Association in 1953, and to the formation of his own psychoanalytic school.

Lacan was never comfortable with the relationship between institutions, including psychoanalytic training schools, and psychoanalysis as a clinical practice. The problem arises because the psychoanalyst helps his patients question their own values and issues, without the analyst having an investment in a particular answer. The psychoanalyst should not bring his own prejudices to bear on his patients' questions. Lacan thought that this special sort of space, in which the patient can speak openly, is essential in psychoanalysis, but very difficult to encourage and promote through an institution because of the kinds of identification and ideals of authority that tend to operate within institutions. Arguing that the institutionalization of psychoanalysis was fraught with dangers for clinical practice, he even took the extraordinary step of dissolving his own psychoanalytic school in 1980, the year before his death.

Lacan's work is difficult to study; not only because he lectured and wrote with a very complicated style, but also because he introduced many new ideas and concepts that are dependent on one another. Studying his work is made more difficult because many of these ideas changed during the course of his lifetime.

Lacan was also an intellectual magpie—he took and adapted for his own ends many ideas from other fields, including linguistics, mathematics, literature, philosophy and science.

Lacan and the Image

One of the main influences on the early Lacan, in the 1920s and 1930s were the Surrealists, then in their heyday. Many Surrealists were interested in psychoanalysis, including Salvador Dali, who met both Freud and Lacan.

In the course of our research we did indeed observe that the mind, once freed of all critical pressures and school bound habits, offered images and not logical propositions

I am not a surrealist

Lacan had noticed that the meanings patients attach to words are often fluid and seem to be attached to images, while meaning in Surrealist art is also attached to images.

How might images play a role in the clinic? Here is an example of someone whose life had been dominated by an image: a woman had a phobia of open and public spaces, so she stayed at home. She had a fear of being seen lying down in the street. In the course of her psychoanalysis it transpired that she was ashamed of her past sexual conduct, and of her sexual desires, and that above all, she did not want to be seen by others as a 'fallen woman'. The image or idea of the fallen woman dominated her life, via the idiom 'fallen woman'. It was around these words that her phobic symptom operated, not only by 'speaking the truth' about her past 'shame', but protecting her from further sexual encounters that she desired.

Here 'fallen woman' is ambiguous, with two meanings, just as Dali's picture on page nine is ambiguous, between a face and women.

In this first phase of his work Lacan stressed the role of images and the imaginary in the workings of the human mind. He had been particularly struck by Lorenz's famous experiment with ducks. Lorenz had put his Wellington boots next to duck eggs. As the ducklings hatched out and saw the boot, they became 'imprinted' with its image; wherever that boot went, the little ducks would follow. They mistook Lorenz's boot for their mummy. When Lorenz wore his Wellingtons he was slavishly followed by a trail of ducklings, each of whom were captivated by the image of the boot.

In the same way, a man might love a woman who looked, smelt or sounded like his mother, because he is captivated by an image of her. It is not unusual for people to fall in love with someone who has something familiar about them, a smell, a laugh or their eyes. In love, we typically confuse our new love with an old love. Lacan once said of his dog:

This idea of 'domination by the image' is for Lacan tied to the concept of captivation, slavery or bondage. Such a bond can exist between a child and mother, between lovers or between a slave and a master.

Lacan took this idea from the German philosopher Hegel, who developed a theory of the 'slave-master relation'. We will look at this in chapter six, on discourse, but to understand the slave-master relation we need to first look at the problems Socrates thought we have in knowing things, and at Freud's theory of consciousness, or the 'ego' which also stresses mis-knowing.

Socrates is an important figure for Lacan because he had a problem with knowing, knowledge, and wisdom, and because he is famous for a special way of speaking and arguing that is now called 'Socratic Discourse'.

Around 399 B.C, Socrates become worried when he heard that:

Socrates was surprised to hear this because he was sure that he was without wisdom. Fascinated by the contradiction between what he thought of himself, and what had been said of him, Socrates went about testing the hypothesis that there was 'no man wiser', by arguing with people who were thought to be wise. He did this by pointing out the contradictions in what people said to him. As you might imagine, this caused a lot of upset and controversy, but it also had a dramatic result, Socrates ended up on trial.

Defending himself, he said that people had become emotionally involved with him because they supposed him to possess knowledge, which in fact he did not have:

'The effect of these debates and investigations of mine, gentlemen, has been to arouse against me a great deal of hostility, and hostility of a particularly bitter and persistent kind, which has resulted in various malicious suggestions, including the description of me as a 'professor of wisdom'. This is due to the fact that whenever I succeed in disproving another person's claim to wisdom in a given subject, the bystanders assume that I know everything about that subject myself. But the truth of the matter gentlemen, is pretty certainly this...

human wisdom has little or no value.'

In the spirit of Socrates, Lacan said that a psychoanalyst has no special knowledge to give his patients. And like Socrates, a psychoanalyst can provide a special kind of logical questioning that can help the person being questioned find some truth about themselves.

You know what is wrong with me. Tell me, what should I do? What job should I do? Who should I marry?

Lacan was interested in the supposition that 'another person possesses knowledge', because that is exactly what happens in psychoanalysis, as well as in some other relationships. The patient who brings his problems and suffering to the psychoanalyst usually supposes that the analyst possesses a special knowledge; typically, knowledge of the solutions to all the patient's problems.

A competent psychoanalyst does not pretend to have such knowledge and, of course, usually has difficulties of his own.

What is at play in this very common supposition of knowledge that patients make of their analysts and their doctors, and that children make of their teachers and parents? Lacan's answer is 'The slave master discourse'.

You're alright, how am I?

More on the slave-master discourse in chapter six.

So one theme for psychoanalysis, from Socrates, is the idea that knowledge is a central problem for each of us, posing difficult questions such as:

What do we know?
How do we know it?
How do we live with it?
How do we speak about what we know?

KNOWLEGE AND DESIRE

In Freud's theory there is—put simply—the unconscious or 'id', where unconscious desires live. It is a safe place for desires that would otherwise embarrass us, or expose conflicts, contradictions and make problems. Consciousness is that part of the mind to which we have access: the images, feelings and ideas that we can simply introspect and see. This, roughly speaking, Freud called the 'ego'. Freud thought of the ego as the surface or façade that negotiates between the unconscious and the world.

How does it do this?

Mostly by a kind of lying, just like Basil Fawlty in the TV show 'Fawlty Towers'. The main job of the ego is to cover over the problematic desires and their conflicts. It does this by making numerous 'false connections' between things, and then making them conscious. For example, a married man explained to a psychoanalyst that his problem was 'alcoholism'. But this man had an unconscious desire to be homosexual, and had used drink as a way of avoiding sex with his wife. He would explain to her 'I can't make love to you because I've been drinking'. It was an explanation that also convinced him. Importantly, it did not betray his unconscious desire to love men, rather than women. His drinking was being used by his ego as a false connection, linking his unconscious desire to love men, with his impotence in relation to his wife.

All his wife saw was his drunkenness and his impotence.

In another example a man, Mr. Jones, fell in love with a married woman, Mrs. Brown. Instead of acknowledging the disappointment of his unrequited love, he slandered the woman's husband, Mr. Brown, spreading nasty rumours about him. The rumours established a false connection between his love, and its disappointment, via his rival.

For Lacan, following Freud, the primary function of the ego, of consciousness, is deception. This means that whatever the circumstances, and however much psychoanalysis a person has had, in matters of consciousness and judgement—

especially reflexive ones in which people make judgements of themselves—the productions of the ego are suspect. Lacan calls the false judgements of the ego 'meconnaissance' or 'misknowing'.

This is a bit like my idea of "bad faith"

I'm so FAT!

The deceptive function of the ego is something that we are all stuck with. A deceptive ego that tells lies is a necessary part of our mental structure.

Freud and Lacan argued that people have an almost infinite capacity to deceive themselves. This is especially true when they are making judgements about themselves, or when they are contemplating their own desire and their own image.

This Freudian model of the 'ego as deceptive' has been confirmed by hundreds of experiments carried out by psychologists with the techniques of mainstream science. But, surprisingly, this Freudian and Lacanian view contradicts what has become the predominant view in American culture and 'therapy': 'Ego Psychology'. What is called 'therapy' in America has very little if anything to do with either Freud's or Lacan's ideas. Ego Psychologists argue that the ego can be 'strengthened', by the construction of a 'conflict-free zone' within it, and thus have the ego 'accord with reality', instead of lying compulsively!

For Lacan and Freud, the ego works to negotiate between reality and unconscious desire by covering up the necessary conflicts that life entails.

In other words, it bullshits, like any public relations department.

Life is tough; we are divided in many ways, for instance as men and women. In our state of division it is far from obvious which is the best way to live. What should we do? Where should we do it? Who should we love? What work should we do? How do we live with our desire? Whatever we do, life is a series of conflicts.

The American dream or ego ideal is that we should eat McDonalds, have 2.3 children and lead good, happy, heterosexual lives without any fundamental difficulties or conflicts. The standard Hollywood solution to life's difficulties, whatever their size or shape, is for a heterosexual man and woman to walk into the sunset holding hands, to make babies. Heinz Hartmann, one of the founders of Ego Psychology, revised Freud's fundamental conception of the ego beyond recognition.

19

Mr Hartmann, psychoanalysis's cherub, announces the great news to us, so that we can sleep soundly—the existence of the autonomous ego. This ego which, since the beginning of the Freudian discovery, has always been considered as in conflict, all of a sudden is restored to us as a central given...the functions of the ego ought, above all else, to encourage us to reexamine certain notions that are sometimes accepted uncritically, such as the notion that it is psychologically advantageous to have a strong ego. In actual fact, the classical neuroses always seem to be the by-products of a strong ego...the real neurotics have the best defenses...

The original Freudian concept of a defensive ego had to be broadened to include in the ego, non-defensive functions of the mental apparatus. Many of these are not, or not necessarily, part of the conflictual set-up; we call them today 'the non-conflictual sphere of the ego'. We speak of the primary autonomous functions of the ego. Through the development of the ego it becomes possible... that the relation between adaptation to outer reality and the state of integration of inner reality has become more accessible.... Ego Psychology represents a more balanced consideration of the biological, social and cultural aspects of human behaviour.

The Ego Psychology ideology suggests a utopia in which we can remove all conflict by seeing 'The Truth' clearly. This view has its roots in Plato's blueprint for a fascist society in which he would expel poets and artists, because 'their art is a deliberate attempt to deceive us, to disguise the truth'. Plato wanted a law ensuring that all single adults over thirty would be fined every year, until they married. He would also encourage adolescent boys and girls to dance together, naked.

So the solution for Ego Psychology as for Plato, is heterosexuality. Ego Psychology claims that truly satisfying sex has to be genital intercourse and can only occur at the end of a successful course of therapy, for those who see 'The Truth'. The guardians of 'The Truth' in Plato's scheme are the elite 'philosopher-kings', the rulers of the state, who have had twenty or thirty years of special 'Truth training' in Plato's doctrine; in Ego Psychology the only ones who are supposed to see The Truth are the therapists and their 'cured patients' who take fifteen or twenty years studying to identify their conflict-ridden egos with the 'conflict-free egos' of their therapists; but for Socrates, Freud and Lacan, life is a disease, and the cure is death.

For Lacan then there is no possibility of living your life **with** conflict and without being misled by your ego, because it is necessarily difficult to be alive. We can only live with conflict. There are profound differences such as gender and sexuality (explored in chapter nine on feminine sexuality) and other problems that cannot be ironed out or eliminated completely by any amount of psychoanalysis, politics or social engineering. Conflict remains an essential part of the package of life. The device that 'manages' the conflict, maintaining a façade, by lying, is the ego. Freud and Lacan argue that we are all in the position, identified by Socrates, of not knowing. Not only do we often not know about reality and the external world in any pure sense, but, more importantly, we may not even know our own deepest desires.

Desires are often unconscious, and are covered over by the false connections of the ego, which deceive us. For Freud and Lacan it does not matter how much psychoanalysis you have consumed, how saintly you are, or for how many decades you have practised meditation, you will still have an ego whose function is to deceive you.

Is the ego in charge then?

No.

If there were an autonomous little man
in charge of the ego, or 'conflict
free ego' as Hartmann claims,
we would have a problem:
what would be inside the
little man's head? The little
man would have to have a
complete mind of his own.
And how would that work?
With its own complete little
man? Would that little man
also have his own little man...?

This problem, with the infinitely many little men, each one smaller than
the one before it is called 'The Homunculus Problem'. We will return to it.
Because it is conceptually impossible, we know that any scheme that relies
on it cannot exist.

Psst! The ego is not master in its own house!

So, in the tradition of Socrates and Freud, Lacan does not believe that we can turn to the ego for answers about our deepest unconscious desires. But there are some linguistic techniques for studying the rewriting and rereading that the ego carries out. However these techniques cannot be relied on to provide us with 'the absolute infallible truth' about ourselves, as Ego Psychologists claim.

In the next chapter we will look at those techniques and at the second stage of Lacan's work, in which he developed and stressed the importance of symbols, of language, rather than the role of images and the imaginary.

CHAPTER 2

WHAT HAS LANGUAGE GOT TO DO WITH PSYCHOANALYSIS?

Before we look at Lacan's and Freud's idea of how language works, and how it dominates our lives, let's start by looking briefly at some very different theories of language and meaning, against which Lacan argued.

Psychoanalysis is carried out exclusively with words, with language. So psychoanalysis, argues Lacan, must have a theory of language and meaning. The surrealists showed that one image can be associated with more than one meaning. But Freud and Lacan claim that meaning is essentially something to do with language, with words and symbols.

Two theories of word meaning:
the
FIXED
and the
Fluid

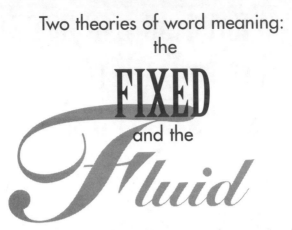

Jung, Klein and Plato had theories of language that are similar: they all claim that some meanings are rigidly fixed and cannot be moved. This position is very different from Freud's and Lacan's view of language, where meaning is in flux.

Jung thought that whatever our experiences, and however different our backgrounds and cultures, we can only conceptualise and experience the world, each other and language through a fixed number of ideas that he called 'archetypes' such as the 'Earth Mother' or the 'Trickster'.

Plato also had fixed ideas that he called 'Forms' such as 'The Perfect Man' and the 'The Perfect Woman'; Melanie Klein's fixed ideas are 'objects' such as the 'good breast' and the 'bad penis'.

But there is a problem with all these theories that insist on having fixed meanings, where one word or image always has one corresponding 'fundamental meaning'. They all run into trouble when it comes to justifying their fixed categories. For instance, one absurd consequence of believing in a theory of fixed meaning is that you could have a 'dream dictionary' that really worked. Such a dictionary would allow you look up 'the definitive meaning' of a dream symbol or image, such as a dog. But if I dream of my dog barking, my dream might have one particular meaning: but if a veterinary surgeon, or perhaps someone with a phobia of dogs, had the same dream, 'dog' would probably have a different meaning. There is no authority, no specialist who 'knows the truth about meaning' and who we can rely on to authoritatively interpret the meaning of our unconscious ideas.

So psychoanalysts are not in a position of authority regarding word meaning either, argues Lacan. The use of a word and its meaning always depends on the user's history and on the use of the word in their life and community. So meaning depends on use, and as use varies, so meaning varies. This is an important idea for Lacan, although he was not the first to have it. Lacan realized that word meaning changes, and depends on other people and on the use they make of a particular word. Let's look in a bit more detail at the ways in which word meaning changes.

It is not possible for one person to decide, on his own, what a word means. If I choose to use the word 'table' as if it meant 'cat', and were to say 'please feed my table while I'm away', and I took my table to the vet, I would soon be corrected.

Word meaning, although it changes over time, depends on all of the people who use the language. Even special scientific words, which seem to be coined by just one famous scientist, only have meaning by virtue of their currency in a whole community of scientists who, in turn, live in the larger, non-specialist language-using-community.

> What does this entanglement of individual and collective meaning imply?

Before answering this question we should look at a technical term that Lacan used in trying to answer the question: 'What is a person?'

The subject, the object, and the signifier

> 'Subject' is an idea that comes from the Ancient Greeks.

They opposed 'subject' with 'object'. This is a bit like making a pair of 'up' and 'down', 'good' and 'bad', 'true' and 'false'. These are called 'logical equivalences' or 'binary opposites'. For Lacan a word's meaning comes from its being contrasted with other words: black with white, hard with soft... This is why a word's meaning changes over time, because it comes to be contrasted with new and different words.

'Subject' and 'signifier' are an important pair of binary opposites in Lacan's theory of the subject. His theory of the subject is, very simply, a theory of what it means to be a person. He argued that we are represented by language, by special objects called 'words'. Lacan's technical term for 'word' is 'signifier'.

PERSON ≈ SUBJECT
WORD ≈ SIGNIFIER

He argued that the signifiers that a subject speaks, writes or dreams, represent that subject.

Or, in Lacan's terms;
'the signifier represents the subject...'

29

> But how is the representation achieved? How is it that a subject gets to be represented by their words?

Whenever anyone speaks or writes they always represent themselves with language, with signifiers. And signifiers are the only way the subject can represent him/herself. So Lacan thought that communication between us is not direct but always mediated through signifiers. This explains why Lacan's slogan is:

The signifier represents the subject for another signifier

Lacan says that 'the signifier represents the subject *for another signifier*' to avoid the homunculus problem (the infinitely many little men, each one smaller than the one before it) that we met in Chapter One. The idea behind this formula is to prevent the subject somehow sidestepping the flow of language, from one subject to another. The flow of language cannot be read from outside language, and language is all with which we can represent ourselves.

Put another way, 'the signifier represents the subject for another signifier' is like saying:

The **lawyer** represents the **client** for another **lawyer**

The **signifier** represents the **subject** for another **signifier**

If you have a legal case against me, your lawyer will communicate with my lawyer. The exchange between us is between lawyers, not directly between you and me.

The two clients will be separated by the legal discourse of their lawyers, which they might not even understand. It is common for lawyers to confuse their clients and to fail to get the best deal for them. So lawyers are separated from their clients by language, but it is only language, including the language of money, that keeps them together. Signifiers both constitute and divide us.

H

ere is another illustration:

'The prime minister represents the nation for another prime minister'. In international relations, it is what the prime minister says that represents me in the international community, whether I agree with him or not. When nations are represented by prime ministers, the views or interests of that nation are often confused, twisted or reformulated. But this, says Lacan, is the relation of the subject to language. We are all alienated by language. Language is the best we can do to communicate, but using it ensures that we will often be misunderstood, however well intentioned our audience might be.

Representation is on a signifier-to-signifier basis, via the medium of the subject: not on a subject-to-subject basis via the signifier.

So, paradoxically, Lacan argues that we are separated and joined by language. It alienates each one of us and yet makes a community of us: a community of alienated and alienating subjects.

Lacanian theory explains the entanglement of individual and collective meanings; you cannot separate subjects from language.

What would humanity be without language?

Lacan had a special vocabulary of technical terms and notations. His abbreviation for the subject is an 'S', but it is not usually written this way, because an essential part of subjectivity is our separation and constitution by language. So Lacan wrote an S with a bar through it, to show our division:

The bar also represents the fact that there is always something stopping the subject from getting what it wants and from being how it wants to be.

I WANT TO BE AN `X`

Theories of language are important for psychoanalysis because psycho-analysis is carried out exclusively with words: the client speaks, and the analyst speaks. For this reason Lacan said:

'psychoanalysis should be the science of language, inhabited by the subject...man is the subject captured and tortured by language.'

And that the dominant part of our minds,

'the unconscious is structured in the most radical way like a language'

What does this mean?
What is the unconscious?
And why did Freud and Lacan believe that the unconscious is the place where hidden desires live?
The answer they both give is

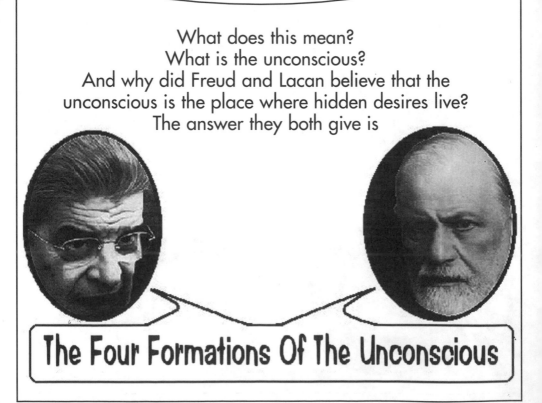

The Four Formations Of The Unconscious

Freud had a catalogue of 'the four formations of the unconscious'. These are four mysterious mental phenomena that Freud took on as a challenge to explain:

SYMPTOMS,
ERRORS OF EVERYDAY LIFE,
JOKES
and
DREAMS.

Freud and Lacan theorised each of these phenomena as linguistic products of the unconscious; as plays of language. Here are some clinical examples:

A SYMPTOM:

The woman from chapter one with a phobia of open and public spaces had a fantasy of falling in the street. In the course of an analysis it transpired that she suffered with guilt and shame, as a consequence of her sexual activity, and did not want 'to be seen as a 'fallen woman". This woman's unconscious desire 'spoke' with a symptom that took the form of an idiom, of language.

AN ERROR OF EVERYDAY LIFE:

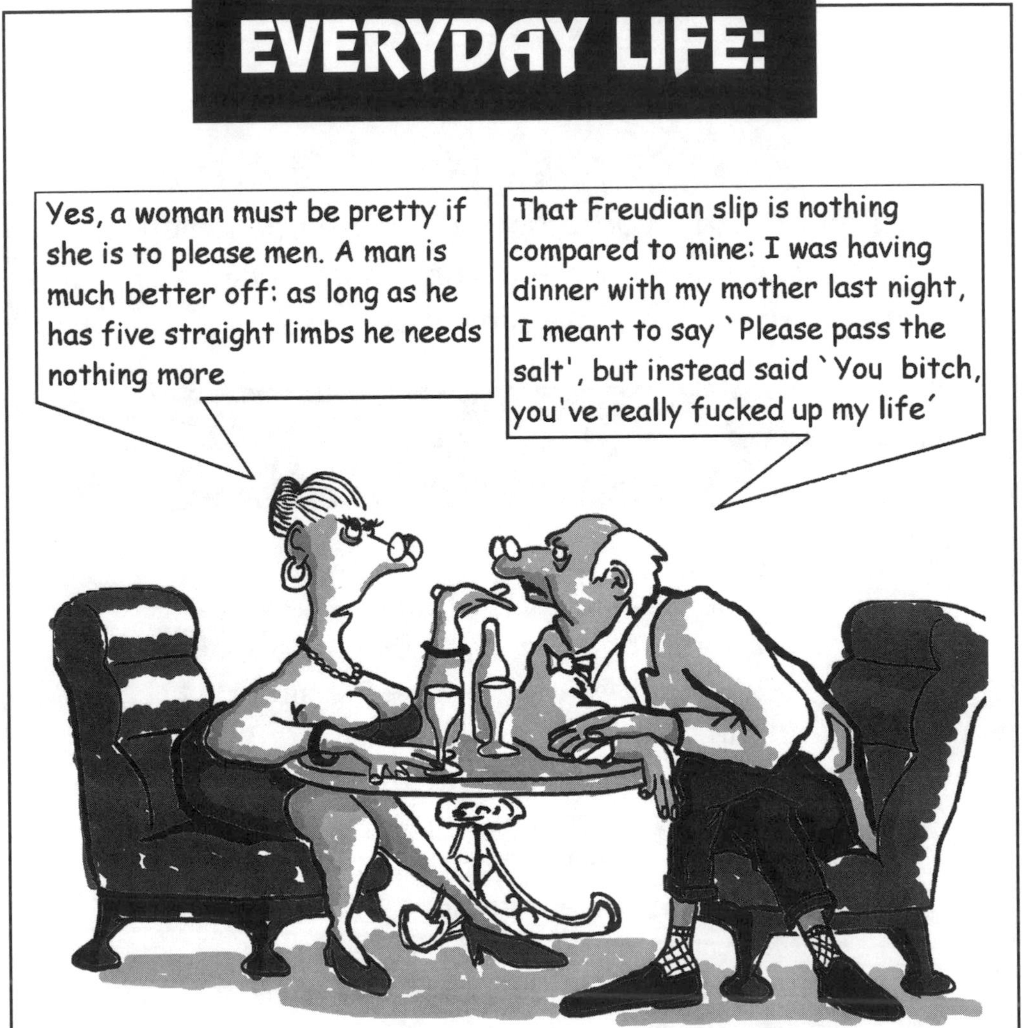

JOKES often have the same structure as slips of the tongue, as we can see in an example of Freud's:

'...a brilliant joke of Heine's, who made one of his characters, Hirsch-Hyacinth, the poor lottery agent, boast that the great Baron Rothschild had treated him quite as his equal—quite 'famillionairely'. Here the word that is the vehicle of the joke appears at first, simply to be a wrongly constructed word, something unintelligible, incomprehensible, puzzling. Accordingly it bewilders. The comic effect is produced by the solution of this bewilderment, by understanding the word. The joke depends entirely on its verbal expression.

Are processes similar to those which we have described here already known in any other field of mental events? They are in a single field, and an apparently very remote one. In 1900 I published a book which, as its title (The Interpretation of Dreams) indicates, attempted to throw light on what is puzzling in dreams. DREAMS EVEN CONSTRUCT [PEOPLE AND THINGS] OUT OF WORDS, AND THEY CAN THEN BE DISSECTED IN ANALYSIS.'

A DREAM:

A young woman felt tied up in her mother's problems and complained that she was having difficulty making progress in her own life. She explained that she had never known her father, and reported a dream in which she was 'being pulled by four bears'. She produced her own reading of this dream: 'forebear' means 'forefather', as well as 'suffer' and 'sacrifice', which appears to refer to what the young woman had given up, in order to continue her difficult relation with her mother.

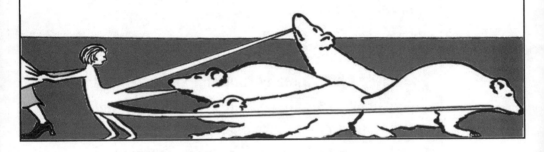

So Lacan understands these four categories: dreams, slips of the tongue, symptoms and jokes as linguistic functions, as the movement of words and letters, as a kind or reading and writing. He called this idea 'The Agency of the Letter', because the letter seems to have a life all of its own, insisting on being rewritten, as the four formations of the unconscious, as signifiers in dreams, jokes, slips of the tongue and symptoms. The letters in books and on gravestones outlive the subject who was spoken by those words.

Now we have looked at how meanings shift about and change, we should return to look a theory which argues that meaning is somehow fixed.

Some theorists called 'sociobiologists' have argued, in the style of Plato, Klein and Jung, that meaning is something that is fixed for people. For these theorists meaning appears to be biologically fixed for us, just as it is for animals and plants. For example, if you wave a red stick at a stickleback it does a mating dance. Red indicates mating for sticklebacks. For them 'red' could never be a metaphor, a symbol, symptom, dream, or a joke because it always refers to one thing and to one thing only. Sticklebacks, argues Lacan, are not divided and structured by language: people are, because the meaning of their words changes.

Lacan argues that meaning is above all a property of language, not primarily a property of biological systems. So looking at biology will not tell you much about the human condition. People are unique: they are the only organism to commit suicide. No other animal kills itself.

The lemming story is a myth.

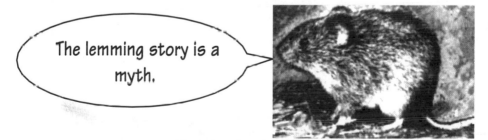

Our lives are radically different from those of all other animals because we are dominated by language, by meaning that is in flux, not fixed.

CHAPTER 3

LACON'S THEORY OF THE

AS THE IMPOSSIBLE TO SAY

By the 1960s Lacan had a broad theory of the psyche or mind, with three different categories: 'the imaginary, the symbolic and the real'. He pictured the three tied tightly together like a knot. The imaginary (in chapter one) is the domain of images, the symbolic (in chapter two) is about language or signifiers: what is the 'real?'

The 'real' is not an account of reality, or the 'objective world' but a kind of recurring impossibility, a 'return of the repressed'. When you read 'real' in this book it is meant in Lacan's sense, not in the ordinary sense. The real for Lacan is 'the impossible to say', or 'the impossible to imagine'. To understand this idea we should look first at a morsel of the history of science:

Reactant
CHO

Thank's to that genius Newton we'll soon be able to measure the universe and understand and predict everything in it

In 1687, the world was being shaken up in a big way by Isaac Newton. People were so impressed by Newton's brilliant theories which, for the first time, accurately predicted the movements of the planets, and all manner of mechanical things, that almost everyone thought that it would only be a matter of time until science could predict all phenomena, the whole universe and everything in it. Man would know everything, and medical science would cure all ills.

It is now widely believed that there are at least three fatal problems with this idea:

1. The first is the problem of how we measure ourselves, measuring ourselves, measuring ourselves, measuring our... This is another version of the homunculus problem.

Or as Lacan said:

> I always speak the truth. Not the whole truth, because there's no way to say it all. Saying it all is literally impossible: words fail. Yet it's through this very impossibility that the truth holds onto the real.

 2. You will have to wait until the chapter on psychosis and 'Godel's Incompleteness Theorem' for the second reason why we cannot 'know everything'.

 Here is the third reason why we cannot have knowledge of everything:

In 1925 another physicist, Werner Heisenberg, had some shattering news. Heisenberg had discovered that it was necessarily impossible to measure some things. He had been trying to measure the position and the speed of an electron as it orbited the nucleus of an atom, whizzing around, like the earth orbiting the sun:

Heisenberg could either find out what the velocity of the electron was, or he could find out what the position of the electron was, but he learnt that he could not find out both. Knowledge of both was **mutually exclusive**. His discovery produced a new attitude to science, with expectations completely different from those of Newton's time. Science could no longer be relied on to solve **all** the problems of life. Since Heisenberg, science, however useful and informative, has become yet another set of impossibilities.

Heisenberg said that the very act of measuring the electron's speed had an effect on it, and so produced the impossibility of knowing the electron's position. So, instead of magically eradicating our impossibilities and our ignorance, science has become a detailed specification of them.

What has all this to do with psychoanalysis, the subject, and Lacan's conception of the real?

The real is that which cannot be symbolised or imagined at a particular time. So for Heisenberg, the real would either be the speed of an electron, or its position, whichever of the two was excluded. Lacan argued that we all endure important impossibilities in our lives. We all face big questions and dilemmas that cannot be avoided, and whichever option we choose, we necessarily exclude others. For instance, being a man, or being a woman entails specific impossibilities for each of us, as does being homosexual, heterosexual, black, white, a parent or childless.

One impossibility we all suffer from is the ideal of perfect communication. We all have to continually endure being misunderstood, misheard and misquoted. We are condemned to use language and to always be misunderstood, whatever precautions we take, even by people who do their best to understand us.

Word meaning is something that seems to be in flux. Word meaning shifts about beyond our control. If you want to know exactly, and without any doubt, what a word means you might try looking up the word in a dictionary. What do you find?

More words, and each of those words has a meaning you can read, but only as more words, and each of these words has a meaning offered by more words... This sea of signifiers with its potentially infinite connections is the same one in which we are each, as subjects, represented.

Gadzooks[1]

Kangaroo[2]

1. ENGLISH LANGUAGE. MEANING; 'WHAT WAS THAT'

2. ABORIGINAL LANGUAGE. MEANING; 'SORRY MATE, I HAVEN'T GOT A CLUE WHAT YOU'RE SAYING'

This view of language argues that meaning comes in packages that are always connected to one another.

culture

language

forbid

NO

WORD

sentence

yes

verb

restrict

message

affirm

Lacan argued that our individual lives centre around what is real for each of us, that is what is impossible to say, and that our individual symptoms—which we all have—are the symbolic expression of what is real for us.

The real is about impossibilities, the impossibilities of language and life. Let's look at the real by returning to the idea of word meanings in flux, with an extreme example, one that we all have some experience of:

TRAUMA

'Trauma' is Ancient Greek for 'wound'.

A trauma is an important impossibility and refers to an experience in a person's life that he has not been able to sufficiently symbolise, or to put into language. Trauma is an experience in the category of the real.

In the talking cure, in psychoanalysis, there is a putting into words, a symbolising of difficulties and traumas. This has the effect of metamorphosing the trauma, of changing the meanings that a particular signifier has for a subject. So 'the trauma' is actually changed by being spoken about. It becomes more clearly symbolised and less real.

Just as measuring the position of an electron means that you have an effect on the electron's speed, so it is possible with psychoanalysis to change what is in the category of the real for a subject, through speech, by getting the patient to talk.

But it is not possible though to remove everything real from the trauma so that it becomes an empty category, containing nothing. We all have to live with the real, with 'the impossible to say'. If we manage to find the words to say something that we could not say before, we can only do so at the cost of introducing new items in the real which we then cannot talk about. Language always introduces new indeterminacies, uncertainties and the renewed division of the subject. This is why Lacan argues that language is a universal trauma or wound, taking a unique form for every subject.

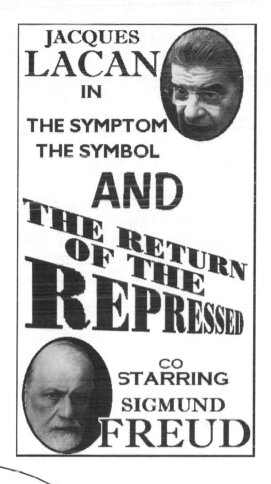

JACQUES **LACAN** IN THE SYMPTOM THE SYMBOL **AND THE RETURN OF THE REPRESSED** CO STARRING SIGMUND **FREUD**

How can you tell what is in the real for a subject?

Lacan says that the real always returns. 'It' comes back, again and again and while each time 'it'—the object of repetition—may be different in some ways, the pattern is the same. Freud had noticed that when somebody had a particularly difficult experience, a 'trauma'—something that they had been unable to speak properly about— that some aspect of their experience would always return.

What form does this return take? It takes the form of the symptom, which is **the return of the repressed**. The trauma always returns in a symbolic form, as language, but is distorted by the ego and repressed, so that it is not consciously recognized. In this way the traumatised subject is 'protected' from coping consciously with their difficulty. Unless you can remember what you had repressed, it will return, again and again to haunt you, in symbolic form.

While 'the return of the repressed' sounds like the title of a ghostly horror film, it describes the patterns we find ourselves repeating. You might find that your love affairs always last until your partner proposes marriage, or that whenever you speak to your grandmother, you don't know why, but you become depressed. Perhaps you always lose your keys on every birthday or anniversary?

The trauma returns in a disguise, as, for instance, the phobia of the woman who feared public spaces, because she didn't want to be seen as a fallen woman, acting on her desire and living with its conflicts. Traumas also return in dreams and slips of the tongue.

We have now glimpsed Lacan's theoretical knotting together of 'the symbolic, the imaginary, and the real'. What are the clinical signs of the real? What is it that is special about symptoms, slips of the tongue, dreams, jokes and fantasies that address the suffering caused by trauma? Lacan's answer to this question is 'jouissance', the topic of the next chapter.

CHAPTER 4

JOUISSANCE
AND ITS RELATION TO THE REAL, THE SYMPTOM, FANTASY AND DESIRE

How can you tell if what you are considering is a symptom or not? In medicine the diagnosis of symptoms is largely a visual matter: the patient is inspected by the trained eye of the doctor.

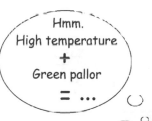

Hmm.
High temperature
+
Green pallor
= ...

In this chapter we will look at a kind of sexual satisfaction that Lacan called 'jouissance' and distinguish it from pleasure. Some other terms are introduced: 'need', 'demand', 'desire', 'symbolic father', 'fantasy' and 'transference'.

The doctor sees the outward images or signs and then infers the identity of the underlying disease.

Medicine

In psychoanalysis diagnosing symptoms is very different. So much so that perhaps the word 'symptom' shouldn't be used for both. First of all, the psychoanalyst doesn't look, he listens.

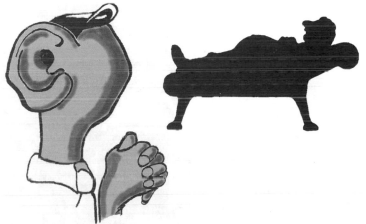

Psychoanalysis

The second big difference is that the psychoanalyst has no diagnostic manual in which he can look up fixed meanings of his patient's words.

Freud was the first to listen carefully to patients, to study their language rather than their images, and to investigate the unique meanings that key words had for each of his patients. He did not make the assumption that he always knew beforehand what his patients' words meant.

This is demonstrated by two patients with exactly the same outward 'symptom', 'anorexia', but each has completely different underlying problems. One anorexic's symptom was her way of trying to communicate her experience of sexual abuse by her father, while the other anorexic saw her mother die painfully of breast cancer and was terrified of becoming a woman with breasts and suffering her mother's fate. So, because of the diversity of human life and language, there **never** could be a diagnostic dictionary of fixed meanings for psychoanalysis as there is for medicine, where meanings are far more fixed.

Psychoanalysis is difficult for clients and analysts, not only because there is no diagnostic dictionary to rely on, but also because it is not always obvious what a patient's symptoms are. A symptom might be any behaviour or experience.

It could be anxiety attacks, a nervous twitch, heterosexual behaviour carried out by a homosexual person, eating olives, working in a bank, anorexia or voting for a particular political party.

The symptom is often something that patients complain about, but it can also be something about which they are unaware. But typically patients complain about their symptoms. They might do this by saying:

I'M FED UP WITH BINGE EATING.

'Why do I always work for bosses who bully me?

WHY DO I LEAVE BOYFRIENDS AS SOON AS THEY SAY "I LOVE YOU?"

I DON'T WANT TO BE CONSTANTLY SEEKING APPROVAL ALL THE TIME.

WHEN I CUT MYSELF, I FEEL A RELEASE, LIKE SEXUAL SATISFACTION.

WHY DO I ALWAYS HAVE AFFAIRS WITH MEN WHO HIT ME?

What do analysts listen for in their patient's language when looking for symptoms? A special kind of sexual satisfaction, excitement or enjoyment that Lacan called 'jouissance'. 'Jouissance' is French for 'coming' as in orgasm. Lacan used this word because he thought that people take a sexual enjoyment in their symptoms, usually secretly. Jouissance is often an unconscious enjoyment. Lacan argued, along with Freud, that people often take sexual satisfaction or jouissance in all sorts of activities that appear to have nothing to do with sexual intercourse. 'Sexual' for Freud and Lacan is a technical term and means far more than sexual intercourse.

People are extraordinarily different from animals in the diversity of things that give them sexual enjoyment or jouissance. People and animals can get sexual satisfaction or enjoyment from smells, images, sensations, but only people can get sexual enjoyment from words, from language, and an extraordinarily diverse range of objects including silk, rubber, black leather jackets and lampposts.

Excuse me!

Animals are relatively straightforward about sex, it has a fixed meaning for them. But some people get sexual enjoyment or jouissance from masturbating with a shoe, some with telephone calls, and some from whipping or being whipped. But it is almost universal for words or signifiers to have an erotic effect, especially when they represent the desire of the other. The most erotic thing for most people are signifiers, hearing another speak their desire.

I WANT YOU

Let's get back to the idea of jouissance as sexual enjoyment, and its connection with suffering. If you ask someone to tell you about their experience of orgasms, usually they will tell you what a wonderful thing orgasms are. But, imagine an experiment: if you were to stop someone having their orgasm just five seconds before they had it, what do you think they would experience?

EXTREME DISCOMFORT AND PAIN

But people don't talk about the discomfort and pain, they only talk about the fun bit that comes afterwards, the jouissance. Now compare this situation with an hysteric (we will find out more about hysterics in chapter seven). Typically the hysteric complains:

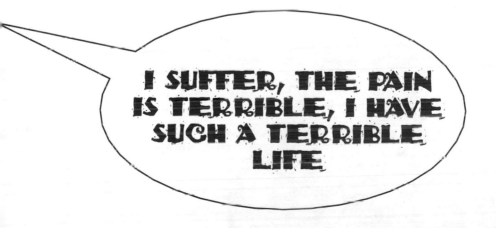

I SUFFER, THE PAIN IS TERRIBLE, I HAVE SUCH A TERRIBLE LIFE

But hysterics won't usually tell you about the satisfaction that they take in complaining. No doubt such hysterics actually suffer pain, but they also enjoy their symptoms. Their enjoyment is usually unconscious: whereas the subject having an orgasm also suffers pain and discomfort, but it is usually unconscious, while s/he enjoys the orgasm consciously. So orgasms are a kind of hysterical symptom with a change of emphasis!

Come again?

The pleasure in sex starts by gradually building, with a linear increase or acceleration of pleasure. Freud called this the 'Pleasure Principle'. When the increase has been well established, the 'plateau phase' begins, when the pain and discomfort start setting in. This pain, which is the interruption of the linear increase of pleasure, becomes increasingly unbearable, until, finally, when the pain is at its height, there is a sudden release of jouissance, of sexual satisfaction.

So the variations of meaning in language, and suffering have all become intertwined with jouissance, with sexual enjoyment. This knotting together of different elements make up the symptom.

	HYSTERIC'S SYMPTOMS	ORGASM
SUFFERING	Conscious	Unconscious
SEXUAL ENJOYMENT/ JOUISSANCE	Unconscious	Conscious

I want my symtoms to disappear!

When someone asks to be psychoanalysed it is usually because they have become aware of some difficulties or problems that they have, and cannot tolerate their suffering. Typically patients say that 'I want my symptoms to disappear'. But it turns out that whatever their symptom is, the symptom is not the patient's fundamental difficulty, but their solution!

The symptom is a clever trick, a compromise that 'speaks the truth' about the patient's trauma and desire, and what is real for them. But it does not speak with a voice that is clear or easy to understand. The symptom encodes, in symbols, what is in the real. In the course of a psycho-analysis, typically taking some years, the meanings of the symbols or signifiers are worked through, and the often complicated meanings of symptoms can become clearer.

So, if a man complained of alcoholism you could waste a lot of time telling him about the health hazards of drink and trying to persuade him to drink less.

In contrast, a psychoanalytic approach would try to understand how drinking solved a problem for him, and more specifically, how drinking might be connected with his suffering. Perhaps then he might be able to change, assuming that he was ready to pay the price of change. It is also possible that when he discovers his reasons for being a drunk, he may prefer to remain a drunk. We will look at this ethical problem of a cure in more detail in chapter eleven which asks:

'What is the Good of Psychoanalysis?'

What the symptom always does is to produce an excitement or jouissance. Jouissance is an attempt at compensation, when the patient tries to 'balance out' his suffering.

Some popular examples are 'comfort eating' or 'comfort shopping' or having lots of short term sexual relationships after the breakup of an important affair.

But as with all symptoms, despite the client's complaints, there always seems to be some jouissance. This enjoyment or jouissance is not the same as pleasure.

JOUISSANCE ≠ PLEASURE

Pleasure and pain are within Lacan's category of **need**. The satisfaction or enjoyment of jouissance does not address needs, such as the need for warmth or food. Jouissance is always a compensation, an attempt to patch up shortfalls in the categories of 'demand' and 'desire' as a way of living with the real.

To get clearer about this we will have to look at how language comes to dominate our existence in more detail, by looking at what Lacan called the 'symbolic father' and the distinctions between 'need', 'demand', and 'desire'.

THE SYMBOLIC FATHER

The symbolic father is not the same as the biological father, whose sperm helped create the subject. Nor is the symbolic father necessarily a man who lived with the subject and played football with him, or her. So what is the symbolic father?

The symbolic father is any agency that separated the young subject from its mother. So for example, if the mother leaves her child to go to work, then mother's work is the symbolic father. If a lesbian lover spends time with the mother, separating the mother from the child, then the lover is the symbolic father. The symbolic father can even be the person who does the mothering, if she is identified as pushing the child away. The separation is regarded by the child as the mother's desire for someone else, for someone other than the child.

How does Lacan's theory of the symbolic father help explain the relation of need, demand and desire? First let's look at three technical terms that Freud and Lacan introduced to psychoanalysis: '**need**, **demand** and **desire**'—they are often confused.

Is that child needy, demanding or desirous?

NEED

'Need' is something physiological such as the need for food or for warmth. Not much about people is simple, but if you could imagine a need on its own—which would never happen—it would be something that could be completely satisfied. If someone is cold, he can be warmed, and if he is hungry, he can be fed. Need in this sense can be eliminated, temporarily.

In this sense people are no different from animals.

A newly born infant is mostly in a state of need. He has sensations of pain and pleasure which are more or less managed by whoever mothers him. Let's call that person the 'motherer', it could be an older brother, sister or the father. So the motherer is the sensation manager of the infant. S/he feeds and changes him, keeping him neither too hot nor too cold, and appearing to the infant to be very much in control of his pain and pleasure. The motherer is powerful in relation to the babies helplessness. Note that this relation of **power over sensations**, of another person's mastery over your pain and pleasure is one definition of sexuality, of love or the erotic.

You make me feel...

As the infant gets older the motherer feeds him less often, but talks to him more. What is she doing? She is feeding her baby words, signifiers. In the meantime the infant quickly gets the idea, from his lack of power, and the motherer's power, that he had better find out what the motherer wants, so that he can give it to her, so that he can continue avoiding pain and getting pleasure. At this point the problem of the real, of impossibility, takes centre stage for the infant.

In order that the infant can be reassured that he is giving his motherer what she wants, as she makes herself increasingly absent, and increases the time between his feeds, he starts learning language, swallowing the signifiers that she has been feeding him. Infants are pressured to speak by their pain and pleasure, by the absence and presence of their powerful motherer. In this way the baby identifies the management of his suffering with his motherer, with the mother tongue.

Shall I be like mummy
or daddy?
Who do I love/hate more,
mummy or daddy?
What do they want from me?
How much do I have to share?
What do I have to give up or
do to get what I need?

Once the child has learnt to speak he has a whole new set of problems that are far more complicated and difficult than the simple needs he started out with. In addition to managing the old problems, his needs, the pain and pleasure, he has new problems: demands, loves and hates, as well as difficulties with ideals, values and ethics. He has problems of conflict with 'the good and the bad', and identifications to make and break. And, crucially, he has to come to terms with the symbolic father, with the other who the mother desires.

What happens after the first phase of need? There is a kind of progression, from need to demand and then on to desire.

DEMAND

'Demand' is a more difficult idea to explain than need. Here is an example of a demanding little boy who says to his mummy:

Can I have some chocolate? Can I have a banana? Can I have a biscuit?

Whatever the boy is physically given, he will ask for something else. What the boy is looking for above all is not an actual object, a biscuit or banana, but an object that does not exist. He is looking for something he will not be given. So he will continue testing his motherer's resources and patience until he finally succeeds in finding something that she will not give. The object of demand cannot exist! For some spoilt children being refused the object of your demand is something that only happens when you have grown up. Until it does you will keep on demanding, and demanding, and...

Note that while the object of need—a sensation—can be supplied completely, the object of demand cannot be supplied at all, because it doesn't exist! Need and demand in this sense are opposites.

There is a popular aspect of demand: love. Demand is always the demand for love. What is love? Loving is being in a state of demand, of wanting to give something that you, the lover cannot give, and wanting to receive something that your loved one cannot give you.

Why are children especially demanding? And why are some adults so demanding? These questions and more are answered in the next section on desire.

DESIRE

Desire is another difficult idea, and, Lacan argued, uniquely human, because it is a property of language. Language is communal property, being owned by no one individual, so each individual desire is part of language. An individual's sexual desire, for instance can often be aroused by a particular form of words, typically those of a potential lover signifying their desire.

...man's desire finds its meaning in the desire of the other, not so much because the other holds the key to the object desired, as because the first object of desire is to be recognized by the other. ...it is ...as desire of the other that man's desire finds form.

I desire your desire for my desire for . . .

Desire dominates our lives and sets us apart from all other animals. Desire is another word for 'lack', for something that is missing: the object of desire. Desire can change its object, and desire often hides—although it will be revealed in dreams, slips of the tongue and symptoms—but it always organises the subject's life in a far more comprehensive way than we ordinarily believe, as we saw in the case of The Fallen Woman.

ere is a review of the terms introduced in this chapter and their relation to each other:

There is a progression, from need to demand and then on to desire. During the first phase of need, the dependency of the child on the motherer is established. In the following phase of demand the child is working in the opposite direction, to separate from the motherer, to separate his desire from his motherer's by placing impossible demands on her that s/he cannot meet. When s/he cannot meet the child's impossible demands, the child's dependence on her has been proved false, and his or her independence of the child's desire has been proved to exist. This proof usually entails the motherer being presented with thousands of fatiguing examples and repetitions of demand. The child reasons:

If mummy cannot give me everything I ask her for then I cannot be dependent on her; I must become independent and find out what is possible for me rather than impossible for her.

Once this proof—that the motherer cannot provide all that the child demands—is sufficiently clear, the child is able to begin to start identifying its own desire; its own desire as separate from its mother's. This is why children are so demanding; their frustrated demand is what gives birth to their desire. Parents identify their own desire out of their frustrated demand with their parents, so desire is the rejection of demand. This is why every generation of parents say:

I always wanted to give you what my parents did not give me

So desire emerges from the child's own frustration, from his demand, addressed to his parents, to which **he** found an inadequate response. Of course each child usually manages to find his own impossible demands. This is why it is naïve to try to give a child everything she asks for. If a child doesn't work through the impossibility of its own demand it will never discover its own desire, and it will demand until it dies. To extinguish demand the child must go beyond it and suffer frustration.

To summarise:

A 'need' is for sensations, that can be 'given'.

'Demand' is for an object that cannot be given.

'Desire' is for an object that can sometimes be reached.

But, if the object of desire is reached, then it no longer remains the object of desire; another object will become substituted in its place.

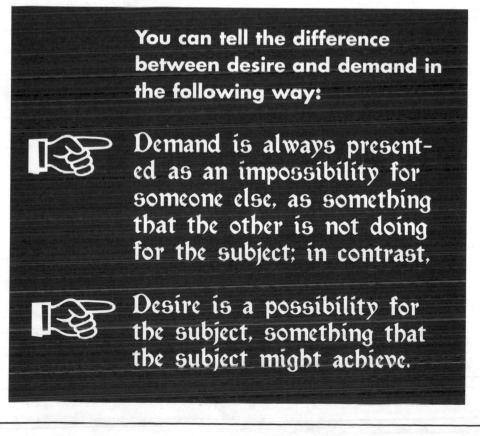

You can tell the difference between desire and demand in the following way:

Demand is always present-ed as an impossibility for someone else, as something that the other is not doing for the subject; in contrast,

Desire is a possibility for the subject, something that the subject might achieve.

In the shifting from need, to demand and on to desire, there is always some residue. All adults obviously continue to have basic needs, although these do not usually seem as urgent to us as they are to young infants. We have to have some needs in order to survive; we need some food and warmth. And demand is also something most of us have at least a minimum of. A minimum of demand is necessary to keep desire going, and for us to love.

If we didn't make demands of each other we couldn't have love affairs or work.

But if you have too much demand, as most of us do, then some of your demand could be metamorphosed to desire. If you have not proved— with your impossible demands— what others cannot do for you, then you will not be able to discover what your own desire is. To find out what you really want in life, to dis- cover your desire, you must have experienced your demands being unmet, some impossibility, an expe- rience in the real. This is one rea- son why life is hard.

You must either suffer your demand or suffer your desire!

When someone has worked through his demand he can speak his desire. Such a person could tell you what they desire and how it drives their life. But many people live in a sort of trance, half asleep, with hardly any idea what they really want. They do not know their own desire and they do not follow it.

But they know best, or at least better than anyone else, what their best course of action should be. Each one of us is The Authority regarding our own resources. If, for example, you live in a homophobic society it may be far easier for you not to recognise your homosexual desire, than to risk rejection by your employer, friends and family. It might be best for you to hide your desire from yourself and others, rather than suffering the consequences of coming out.

For such people who do not act on their desire—most of us—jouissance is the compensation we provide for ourselves, through the symptom. The symptom makes jouissance, and is a tortured compromise between the demand for love, and the desire to speak the truth of unconscious desire plainly, so that everyone will understand.

A subject's demand for love can never be properly articulated because demand, or love, is for an object that does not actually exist. This is why love has always been such a popular theme of songs, poetry and art throughout history.

Love is inexhaustible, because its object cannot be grasped.

THE WORKINGS OF DESIRE

In this section we will look at the ways in which pleasure, desire and jouissance are not fixed but in flux—because of their relation to language—and how the fantasy works to keep desire going by using a fixed idea.

The infant according to Freud is 'polymorphously perverse'. He meant by this that the ways in which the infant can derive pleasure and satisfaction or jouissance are not fixed, but can vary enormously. There are infinitely many forms that can provide pleasure and satisfaction, but as the child ages, the sources of his pleasure and satisfaction become increasingly fixed. All pleasure for the infant is in relation to the motherer and the symbolic father, so pleasure takes on a relation to language, to signifiers.

What piece of speech *doesn't* have some kind of sexual innuendo?

Adults too have an extraordinary range of sources of sexual satisfaction including words, breasts, specific smells, hair, genitals, rubber, animals, a particular voice, a kind of look... But as time passes the source of jouissance, or the object of desire becomes increasingly fixed.

The list of objects of desire for infants is infinite, because sexuality is not fixed for people as it is for animals. Remember that if you wave any red object at a stickleback, at the right time of the year, he will do a mating dance. That is what 'red' means to a stickleback. It has one and only one fixed meaning. Because people have language, and because we can mate all year round, meaning is in flux, especially sexual meaning.

The meaning of sex is not fixed by the seasons or reproduction. In fact, it is often very difficult to separate meaning and sexuality when people are concerned, but not so with the other animals.

The world is a very chaotic place for infants, where meaning is not fixed. In the whole animal kingdom human infants are the most disorganised and most helpless, for the longest period. If you compare a baby with a dog, an ant or an elephant at six months, or at any time up to five years, it is the human who is the most helpless, the most dependent.

If I gave you a very thick book and told you that 'This is a list of every sentence in English'. You would probably say, correctly: 'No it's not, I can add another, and another and...'

The fact is that there is a potentially infinite number of sentences in English, or in any language. You probably speak a brand new and unique sentence at least once a week. So how do we get to learn the rules, the grammar for speaking and understanding this infinity of sentences that could never possibly be learnt by rote? The answer in brief is 'repression'.

Repression is a technical term for 'learning'. In order to express yourself, to use language and to be understood, you must use rules, the rules of grammar, of word meaning, at least most of the time. And 'the learning of rules' is repression. For a subject to follow and obey a rule is for that subject to be repressed. We saw earlier that some of this repression comes from the motherer, from the mother tongue, from a kind of torture where the infinitude of language and jouissance take the place of pain and pleasure, and of the fixed meanings that animals have.

How can infants who are so helpless, learn something as complicated as language, with an infinity of sentences, in such a short time?

What do you mean 'an infinity of sentences'?

To express yourself in language you must have learnt the rules of grammar and word meaning. So repression and expression are two sides of the same coin. In order for there to be an expression, there must have been repression. So, for example, it is now common in Europe and America for Jews to assimilate, to become absorbed into the culture of the country that they live in. To do in Rome as the Romans do. Typically such Jews do not practise their religion, and they often marry non-Jews. But if there was to be a strong resurgence of anti-Jewish racism, with Jews being murdered and treated badly, you could be sure that there would be a renewal of Jewish culture, and a failure to assimilate. Many 'Jewish atheists' would find God, and there would be a return to the old traditions.

So the expression of Jewish culture depends on its repression, on the ways in which it has been learnt.

Sometimes there is too much repression which is called 'trauma', and sometimes there is too little, which is also a problem. There is probably hardly ever just the right amount of repression; so most of us are neurotic. Patients in psychoanalysis have either too much or too little repression. In both cases there is always some surplus demand, waiting and nagging to be metamorphosed into desire.

WHY?

Desire is always desire for another's desire

Here are two different but related ways of answering this question. The first is a bit abstract:

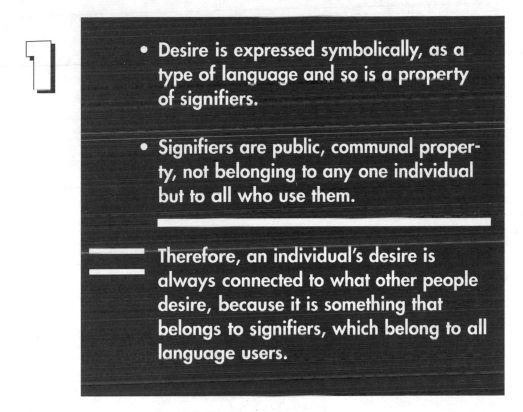

- **Desire is expressed symbolically, as a type of language and so is a property of signifiers.**

- **Signifiers are public, communal property, not belonging to any one individual but to all who use them.**

Therefore, an individual's desire is always connected to what other people desire, because it is something that belongs to signifiers, which belong to all language users.

This conclusion may seem absurd because we are used to the idea that our desires are private, not public. Certainly we can hide our desires from others and from our own consciousness. But if I hide my desire from myself then it will find some other way of 'speaking'. Desire always uses signifiers to express itself. Whether or not you are aware of it, or consciously willing, you will be spoken by your signifiers—and if you don't speak them, they will speak you, in a slip of the tongue, in a dream or as a symptom.

2

Desire is desire for difference

The child's demand is always addressed to an other, or m/other, to those who care for him, so the desire that grows out of the child's frustrated demand is always in relation to others, and to the language of others, because it was the other who frustrated the child and fed him words instead of pleasure.

Why did Lacan say that 'desire is desire for difference?' The object of demand is that which the other cannot give. So the child of poor parents might demand money from them, while the child of wealthy parents might demand that they tolerate his poverty-stricken appearance, ragged clothes and lack of interest in being respectable.

I'm going to be whatever you don't want me to be

I must warn you, Sir, that if you give me another detention then you will just be driving me back into my old ways!

The orientation of the child's demand is in the opposite direction to what his parents ask of him. This is because parents tend to resist some of their child's demands, and so the child's desire is always the efficient establishment of difference, in relation to his parents' demand or desire.

Lacan's Theory of Fantasy and Transference

What does fantasy do? The most important function of fantasy is to help keep desire going. Desire is the stuff of life, the most important fact of human existence. How does fantasy help maintain desire? By fixing.

Is it because many women have fantasies of making love in public spaces, that most people with phobias of public spaces are women?

Usually a subject's fantasies are close variations on a single theme. Lacan called the underlying fantasy that generates these variations the 'fundamental fantasy'. Because the subject's fantasies are all similar they have the effect of minimizing the variations in meaning, which might otherwise cause a problem for desire. Here is one example: if you desire your lover, but your lover is on the other side of the planet, what do you do? Why does your desire not disappear, in the absence of its object? How do you prevent your desire flagging? You wheel in a special mechanism: fantasy. You fantasize that you are with your lover.

So fantasy operates to keep desire roughly constant, to protect it from too much variation. Having your object of desire too far away is one problem: having it too close is another. Sometimes, when the object of desire has been too close, or present for too long, desire can begin to flag. Witness the fading of sexual interest that lovers often have in each other after years together. Desire in these cases can be maintained via fantasy. Typically such lovers fantasize—sometimes unconsciously—that they are having sex with someone other than their partner. Some evidence for this is the common use that lovers make of pornography. As Freud put it:

I am accustoming myself to regarding every sexual act as a process in which four individuals are involved

'Transference' is a kind of translation. In transference an image or idea of the subject is projected onto someone else who is not the original love object. There is also a transfer of love or hate and supposed knowledge to a new person, of the sort that had Socrates put to death. If a man's mother had a big nose, he may marry a woman with a big nose because he 'mistakes' his wife for his mother; he transfers or translates his love for his mother to his wife.

This leads us to another fundamental concept of Freud's that Lacan developed— 'transference'.

When Lacan said:

> I love Justine, my bitch, because she never mistakes me for anyone else.

He meant that whenever there is love, there is always a mistaken identity, because when there is love there is demand, and demand is for something that does not exist. With the first love, between the motherer and infant, the powerless infant imagines that there exists some special object, something which will maintain his relation with the powerful motherer. All other love relations that follow from this first one seem to be based on it. Every consequent love relation appears to be an attempt to reproduce what the infant believes he once had in his relation with his motherer. What is this object, that is so important for infants, and what is its relation to desire? Lacan's answer is that it is 'a fiction', something that does not actually exist except as a kind of convention, but that does not stop us looking for it!

Now we have looked at jouissance, the symptom, fantasy, need, demand, desire, and the symbolic father, we are ready to explore Lacan's theory of the other and the object, and their relation to the subject.

CHAPTER 5

OBJECTS AND THEIR SUBJECT

The object of psychoanalysis is not man; it is what he lacks - not an absolute lack , *but the lack of an object*

Just as there is a subject in Lacan's theory, so there are 'objects'. 'Subject and object' are a strange kind of pair that are always entangled with one another. What is an 'object' in Lacan's theory, and how does it relate to the subject and to subjectivity? Just what did Lacan mean by 'object'?

He doesn't mean a physical object such as a table or brick but something that has a special importance for a subject's desire. For any particular subject there are a variety of possible objects. But you do not 'collect objects until you have a complete set'. In such a theory a subject would collect his objects and all would then be well, for he would be whole. Just like a chess set would be whole when all its pieces or objects are assembled. But Lacan does not believe that a subject can 'be whole', but rather that subjectivity is about there being something missing. It is 'the something missing' that is the object, in the way that an empty place setting at a table suggests a lack, or a scar on someone's face recalls an absent knife. The subject is made up of absent objects, of things missing and lost, and often imagined by the subject to reside in others, in other people. This is why it is usually pleasing to be told: 'I missed you'; it tells you that your being missing (as an object) has something to do with the other's fantasy and desire.

S/he has or is my missing object, and will make me whole.

Objects circulate around the subject and only achieve a proper resting place in death. Even in death some objects such as—'words'—the signifiers spoken or written by the subject, often live on.

When you love someone—in whatever way—you take some aspect of them as an object. But however much empathy or sensitivity you have, you cannot have another subject's experiences or subjectivity. You can only respond to the other's image or their signifiers.

It is not possible to have another subject's experiences—which are probably unique—but only to have one's own subjectivity. So the other can never properly identify 'another subject exactly like me', but only an other, a kind of object.

So women are objects for men: men are objects for women: men are objects for men, and women are objects for women. Each of us can only ever be objects for another subject, however much we try, because we are all separated by language. The only thing that can be a subject is that unique subject, in relation to his language, to his signifiers.

For the woman there is something unacceptable, in the fact of being placed in the position of an *object* in the symbolic order, to which, on the other hand, she is entirely subjected *no less than man*

Men need to spill their seed; we're just their objects, their things their means to an end. I tell you this: they almost never look me in the eye. They can't do that, you see? They can't think of me as a woman, a real human being, `cos what would that say about them?

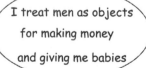

I treat men as objects for making money and giving me babies

All of our identifications and differences with one another, whatever our gender, are produced through images or signifiers, that is through a kind of object. The idea of a subject is paradoxically both dissolved and constituted in an ever-changing set of images or signifiers. This is why Lacan says:

> The signifier represents the subject for another signifier.

Here is an incomplete Lacanian catalogue of objects:

- The **'Names-of-the-Father'** is crucial in understanding psychosis, the theme of chapter eight.

- **Words or 'signifiers'**. These both divide the subject, and make up the subject, for instance as 'the symptom which speaks', for example, in the Fallen Woman's phobia of being publicly seen as 'fallen'.

- The **phallus** (which is not same as the penis) is considered in chapter seven.

- The **'little object'** as the object of desire and the cause of desire. Sometimes known as the 'little other'.

- The **'big other'**, that is, the other of language

Now we have looked at signifiers, it is time to look at two different kinds of Lacanian object: the 'little other', and the 'big other'.

The little object, as the object of desire and the cause of desire

This little object or little other is a remarkable thing, because, above all, it is not 'a thing' in the usual sense, and because it is so important. It is important because it causes desire. It causes or starts desire. There is something necessary about the cause that has the effect of desire. To explain this we should look at the difference between 'causes' and 'reasons'.

'Causes' distinguished from 'reasons'

'Cause' should be radically distinguished from logic or reason. If, for example, the rules of chess are being explained to you, it would be extremely unhelpful to have a move explained by appealing to 'causes':

> Bishops move diagonally because of electrical and chemical reactions in the player's nervous system

Bishops move diagonally because that is the rule by which they operate as a matter of convention or logic, not as a matter of causality. We could just as well move bishops like castles, in straight lines, or move castles in diagonal lines. Of course, actually moving chess pieces involves the body, with its electrical and chemical reactions, but there are no obvious causal issues of physics or chemistry here, only issues of rules and how they are followed. They are a matter of logic, reason or rules, not causes.

> If, on the other hand, you took your car to be fixed and the mechanic said that there were no mechanical issues causing problems with the car, only logical ones, you would probably change your mechanic, quickly.

Logic, or the rules about language and truth, is a different type of language from the language of causality used in science. This brings us to what is special about the little object, the little other: it is both the object of desire—which is a logical item—and it is the cause of desire, which is a causal item.

With the example of an object of desire, such as the voice: you might have first been caused to desire by your mother's voice, when she spoke to you as an infant. As an adult you may then desire someone whose voice is similar to your mother's. So the voice would be the object of desire, as well as its cause. In this case the same thing, the voice, traverses both types of terrain, the causal and the logical. The little object appears the same but our relation to it takes completely different forms, causal and logical. This is one reason why love and desire are so complicated; they are governed by two different languages: logic or rules, and cause.

The little object is somehow in no mans' land, between the subject and the big other of language. The little object is the demand or desire of the other, as taken up by the subject. So examples of the little object include the voice and the gaze of the other. We make others aware of our desire through our gaze, and the sound or tone of our signifiers.

What does your looking at me like that mean?

That tone of voice means that she wants me...

The big other, the other of language

This is an easier idea. While the little object includes images of the other, the big other is the other's signifiers, but at the level of logic and meaning, not at the level of cause.

The big other takes on board Lacan's idea that 'desire is the desire for the other's desire', because language is the privileged expression of desire. Whenever we speak and signify our desire we find ourselves in the other's language, because 'the signifier represents the subject for another signifier'.

The big other—which can be the mother—is particularly associated with the mother tongue at the level of meaning, but not its tone, grain or accent, which are closer to the little object. The big other is taken up for example, in the description of the subject's body by the other. There is an interesting exploration of the little other and its relation to the big other in the infamous film 'Peeping Tom', in which a film maker, as he filmed, would stab his victim with the end of his tripod. But there was a mirror attached, reflecting the victim's look of terror, so his victims could see themselves dying. The victim then experienced the sight of his own death as if from the other's viewpoint.

So the subject in this film, the victim—in his death—takes himself as an object, just as the big other does.

This is a dramatic version of a common experience: the uncanny effect of listening to one's own voice, as if from the position of the other, through the speaker of a tape recorder

The fascination of these scenes arises because they underline the fact that the images we have of ourselves are always very much connected with language, with the other's signifiers. So, you may believe, for instance, that you have pretty knees, or a big nose; not simply because you decided one day, without reference to your culture and community of images and signifiers, completely on your own, that 'my knees are pretty' or 'my nose is big', but because, over the years, people have commented and compared, if not on the feature that you have judged, then on one similar to it, or a related theme. Our own judgement and the image of our own bodies seems to be very much filtered through language, through our own local and family culture.

One dramatic bodily symptom is 'stigmata', the bleeding hands that some Christians present, especially around Easter. Stigmatics bleed from the palms, where, in paintings and sculptures, it is culturally designated that Christ's body was pierced. But if you were to try attaching a man to a cross, by driving nails through his palms, the nails would just tear through his hands and he would fall off. The Romans were not so stupid, their nails went through the wrist. But is that where stigmatics bleed? No, stigmatics bleed from the place where they imagine Christ to have bled from. So their symptoms are addressed to an other, as a demand, an appeal to the other's desire in the form of a symptom.

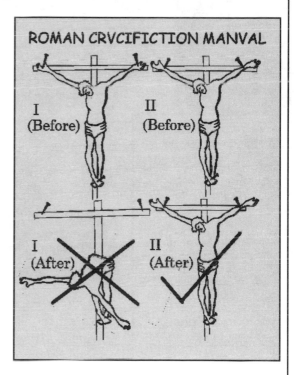

ROMAN CRVCIFICTION MANVAL

I (Before)   II (Before)

I (After)   II (After)

The subjectivity of a stigmatic has something to do with his image of Christ, and the way that it addresses what lacks in his life, that is his desire.

To sum up this chapter: the object or other is always a lack, something missing, from which subjectivity, desire and meaning arise.

CHAPTER 6

LACAN'S THEORY OF THE FOUR DISCOURSES
FOUR WAYS OF SPEAKING & BEING

Here is an example of people, apparently 'communicating':

Isn't it windy?

No its Thursday

So am I, let's go and have a cup of tea.

What is 'communication?' Not the straightforward passage of language. It seems that there is always some addition, subtraction or variation, as the game of Chinese Whispers demonstrates. What people often do with language, it seems, is to misunderstand each other, especially in matters of love.

What is the relation of people to language? In Lacan's theory the subject is divided, above all, by language. Language, as we have seen, fails each of us, and constitutes our subjectivity, that is what makes us human. Through language we misunderstand and are misunderstood.

The only way in which a subject can be undivided or 'whole', is for a very short time, by having jouissance, and we have seen that jouissance always comes in a package with problems, with suffering, conflicts and subjectivity.

In exactly what ways is the subject divided by language or discourse? Lacan believed that there are at least four different ways of being with language, four kinds of relation or discourse.

WHAT ARE THE FOUR DISCOURSES?

e've only got time to look at the slave-master discourse; it is the first and so the most fundamental of all four of Lacan's discourses. Society could survive without the 'discourse of the hysteric', and that of 'the analyst', as well as without 'the discourse of the university', but we must be slaves and masters because we have competition, children and parents.

Lacan's understanding of the slave-master relation was developed from Hegel's theory. The main variables for Lacan are recognition, desire and jouissance. The slave, because of his subjectivity and loss, has some chance of reflecting and recognising his own desire: the master has far less chance of recognising his desire because he pressures the slave to recognise his **demand** for enjoyment. For Lacan the slave-master relation is universal, one in which we have all invested, either as slaves in some voluntary sense or as masters. As slaves we can enjoy the comforts of having a master, as a domestic pet does its human owner. As masters we can deceive ourselves about our desire by distracting ourselves with slaves whose purpose is to provide us with jouissance or enjoyment. This, to some extent, is the relation of parents to their child.

'We live in a society in which slavery isn't recognized. It's nevertheless clear to any sociologist or philosopher that it has in no way been abolished....bondage hasn't been abolished, one might say it has been generalized. The relationship of those known as "the exploiters", in relation to the economy as a whole, is no less a relationship of bondage than that of the average man. Thus the master-slave duality is generalized within each participant in our society.

'The master has taken the slave's jouissance from him, he has stolen the object of desire as object of the slave's desire, but at the same time he has lost his own humanity. It was in no way the object of jouissance that was at issue, but rivalry as such. To whom does he owe his humanity? Solely to the slave's recognition. However, since he doesn't recognize the slave, that recognition literally has no value. The one who has triumphed and conquered the jouissance becomes a complete idiot, incapable of doing anything other than having jouissance, while he who has been deprived of it keeps his humanity intact. The slave recognizes the master, and thus he has the possibility of being recognized by him.'

Lacan argues that slavery and mastery operate universally in the mind and society. Democracy is a popular solution to political injustice but democracy does not eliminate slavery and mastery, it merely disguises it. In general people slave to be masters. Those who regard themselves as slaves suppose 'their masters' to possess knowledge and to have special access to jouissance. Many of those deemed to be 'masters' also promote the propaganda that they have knowledge and power, and hold the solution to the slave's problems. The resulting slave-master relation is a collusion, a drama of compounded fictions. Each master is a slave to his own mastery. So the warders in a prison are a kind of prisoner too, confined in almost exactly the same way as the convicted prisoners.

The idea and practice of being a slave is always entangled with the idea of being a master: the idea and practice of being a master is always entangled with the idea of being a slave. In the slave-master discourse jouissance is a central issue because infants and motherers both play at being slave-master, because the motherer-infant relation is the prototype for future adult sexual relations.

A child sucking at his mother's breast has become the prototype of every relation of love

Slavery in the motherer-child relation arises from the suffering of pain by the child at what it understands to be the powerful hands of the masterful motherer. Who is in control of absence and presence in peek-a-boo games? Is it the baby as he gazes at the mother, then diverting his gaze, or is it really the motherer who actually has far more power to leave? For the baby, the motherer has the masterful position (she plays with her presence and absence by allowing her child a pretend mastery) but the mother may believe that her baby (which she chose to have) has made a slave of her.

In a slight caricature: those who identify themselves as slaves, including prisoners, children, husbands, wives, employees, and those in any service industry usually believe that their master has all the fun, all the jouissance; while paradoxically those who identify themselves as masters usually believe that the slaves have a privileged access to jouissance. Sometimes slaves say that they are getting a fair deal, but they will usually complain at the earliest opportunity and try to better their deal with their master.

Negroes are sexual athletes. My sort give them a rough time but they have more fun in bed than us.

One demonstration of the importance of jouissance in the slave-master relationship can be seen in submissive-domination sex enjoyed by so many, and in the popular erotic literature on the jouissance 'of slaves and masters' that details who takes jouissance from whom, and how much. It is no coincidence that black people are sometimes regarded by whites as taking more enjoyment from sex than themselves.

Class divisions show a separation of the upper class and working class, both of whom believe the other to be stealing jouissance from themselves. Look at plays like 'Oleanna' (Mamet) or 'Miss Julie' (Strindberg) which dramatically switch around the roles of slave and master, or at the TV series 'Upstairs Downstairs'. Each of these works illustrate the slave-master discourse: when the class or race barrier that holds jouissance in place is threatened by an interclass marriage, all hell breaks loose; the reassuring structure of mastery and slavery is in danger, as the economy of jouissance threatens a revolution.

'Staff are most fortunate; they do not suffer restrictions on their personal leisure pursuits, nor endure the moral obligations that we must uphold'

'We do all the work: them upstairs have all the fun.'

Because slaves and masters have so much invested in the system that expresses and represses their desire, which both allows and forbids their jouissance, or their symptoms, it is common for both to show extreme loyalty or bondage to their slave-master culture. So much are the two entwined that it is often difficult distinguishing the slaves from the masters. This is one reason why revolution is so difficult to achieve: the oppressed have often become unconsciously invested in their repression.

'Sisters, why do you allow yourselves to be enslaved in the bondage of marriage?'

Distinguishing slaves from masters is not possible. Nor is it possible, Lacan argued, to distinguish the healthy from the sick as we will see in the next chapter.

CHAPTER 7

FREUD'S AND LACAN'S CONCEPTION OF PSYCHOPATHOLOGY, *OR* WHAT IS HEALTHY AND NORMAL AND WHAT IS NOT?

Working with Freud's ideas, Lacan identified a comprehensive set of diagnostic categories or 'psychic structures'. There are four different structures: hysteria, obsessional neurosis, perversion and psychosis.

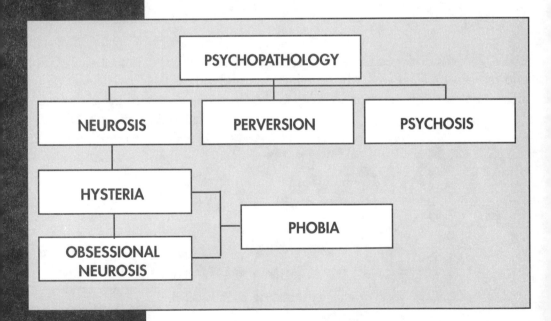

Lacan thought that your psychic structure would tend to be dominated by one of them—but that psychosis is different. But more of that in the next chapter. In this chapter we will look at hysteria and obsessional neurosis, the two kinds of neurosis.

Medicine

Those with neurotic structures sometimes have some insight into their problems, although typically not much. They often have some beliefs along the lines that their symptoms have something to do with their suffering and some awareness of the contradictions in their life, loves, and desires.

Psychoanalysis

But a diagnosis cannot be 'read off'' from a person's behaviour or appearance in any simple way, as it often is in medicine. Two people who cut their wrists, or two alcoholics may have totally different psychic structures; to discover which of the four structures dominate a particular subject, an analyst would have to study the subject's language, rather than his outward behaviour or image. In medicine it is standard practice to infer disease states from the outward appearance; not so in psychoanalysis, where words have unique meanings for each speaking subject.

Given that symptoms can take any form, and that any symptom can have any meaning/s, what is the psychoanalytic idea of health or a cure? In Freud's and Lacan's theory life itself is pathological, disease. What does 'disease' mean in general? Certainly disease only afflicts things that live. But disease is not something that **may** happen to living things; disease is a necessary condition of life, for all living things. Everything that lives is necessarily diseased.

The various problems that get so much attention from psychoanalysis are not just suffered exclusively by just a few diseased people but by all of us. There is no human being who is not either neurotic, psychotic, or perverse.

It's all here in in my little book

THE PSYCHOPATHOLOGY OF EVERYDAY LIFE

This way of thinking is radically different from most American therapies or from the school of Ego Psychology where the practitioners claim that after completing their treatment you will end up 'healthy, with your ego telling you the truth about reality'. For Lacan and Freud the four different pathologies describe humanity as it is: there is no fifth category of 'health'!

'Healthy' is not a category; life is dis-ease, conflict, and there is no way of avoiding it. The question is, how do you choose to live with your conflicts, with your desire? What form does your dis-ease take: neurosis, psychosis or perversion?

Do not forget—when I am dead—sacrifice a cock to the god of healing for me.

Now let's have a look at hysteria, a kind of neurosis.

SOCRATES

The Structure of
HYSTERIA

In hysteria there is one main desire that the hysteric does not properly recognise as his or her own. They do this by overemphasizing the importance of other people's desires, and by underemphasizing their own. So a hysteric might complain:

> Without you, I am nothing.

> 'He wants this from me, and she wants that...

> They are all placing their demands on me. Why does everyone want so much from me when I want nothing from them?

A hysterical car driver might imagine that every single horn she heard was a critical response to her driving. Hysterics will prefer to talk about what other people in their life want—especially of them—while they play down what they really desire for themselves. Often the hysteric's symptoms include some psychosomatic complaint, that is some bodily pain or suffering. Perhaps headaches, blindness or a phantom pregnancy in which an abdomen really swells up, but with an imaginary foetus.

One of the main functions of psychosomatic symptoms is to be an address to the other, like a letter. The symptom speaks the hysteric's desire and demands to be addressed by the other. It calls out for a response and for interpretation from the other; the Fallen Woman's phobia, in the first chapter, is an example of the hysteric's symptom as the demand for the other's desire.

The hysteric won't usually be quiet about his discomfort or pain, typically he will limp about making his suffering obvious, or complaining to complete strangers. Hysterics with psychosomatic symptoms almost certainly suffer discomfort and pain. They may be 'making up' their symptoms in some sense but that does not mean that they are not suffering.

HYSTERIA

MUM ASHAMED OF SEX CHANGE SON

DEAR MARJE

FOR as long as I can remember, I have wanted to be female. I hated my male body, my penis and testicles. I began wearing women's clothes secretly in my teens. Though I looked genuinely male, I was totally... been a it... difficult haus... huge problems with family and friends.

Most hysterics are women, and most obsessionals are men. But beware! Meaning is very much in flux for people, including the meaning of gender; 'a man' is not necessarily someone with a penis, nor is 'a woman' necessarily a person with a uterus, as pre-operative transsexuals complain.

I am a woman

Preoperative transexual man

I know I have the body of a weak and feeble woman, but I have the mind and stomach of a king

Lacan made a distinction between the type of genitals a person has, and their psychic structure; a person with a penis may have a woman's psychic structure, and a person with a womb can be man.

Queen Elizabeth I

This point is supported by the fantasies people have; one common fantasy, for men—for those who typically have penises—is 'having sex with men'. And a common fantasy for many women—I mean mostly for those with a uterus—is: 'I am a man'.

Fantasies are important in any attempt to understand sexuality because desire arises out of difference, above all from sexual difference. So one important question for the hysteric identifying his desire—from within the confusing field of sexual difference—is:

I am a man

I want to love/ have sex with men

How is it that I am desired by the other? Actively or passively? Am I a man or a woman?

It is also common for daughters to identify with their fathers, and to become in some ways like their fathers, and for sons to become like their mothers. The questions: 'What is male' and 'What is female?' do not have obvious answers, nor do they simply focus on a subject's genitals, as we will see in the chapter on feminine sexuality. Human sexuality is not 'a given value', a thing of fixed meaning but something that is a part of the infinite diversity of culture and language. Sexuality therefore has a symbolic value, and is more determined by language than the genital type.

OBSESSIONAL NEUROSIS

For the obsessional there is often a different fundamental question from the hysteric's question. The obsessional asks:

> Am I alive or dead?

What sort of clinical picture and symptoms do obsessionals present? A typical complaint might sound like this:

> On the one hand... but on the other... Nothing changes in my life. I do this very long and complicated task, but it's impossible, it doesn't get me anywhere, so I try and do this other impossible task, and then I go back to the first, and then... I have trouble choosing...

Children usually go through obsessional games, rituals and phases, these might include touching everything made out of wood, or insisting that they do not step on lines. Adult obsessionals often exhaust themselves with similar activities as well as: compiling endless lists, having a lot of trouble finishing anything, and amassing huge collections, which are also, usually, unfinished, with one or two stamps or matchboxes that remain missing. As a matter of course they get horribly tangled in labyrinthine impossibilities and become unable to decide, one way or another, on a course of action that would lead them out of their mess.

At the heart of an obsessional's symptoms—his fundamental fantasy—is not one hidden desire, which the hysteric has, but two. The two desires are believed by the obsessional to be mutually exclusive, that is, they are 'in the real'. They are desires whose individual goals rule each other out.

99

Here is a famous clinical case from Freud known as 'The Rat Man'. He was a young man who was a daddy's boy and wanted his father's approval for whatever he did. And he wanted to marry his girlfriend, but his father disapproved of the girlfriend;

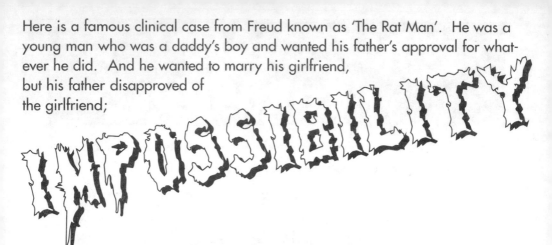

IMPOSSIBILITY

Either the young man was to follow his love for his girlfriend, or to follow his love for his father. This obsessional's two mutually exclusive desires are:

1. To have the love and approval of his father, who disapproves of the girlfriend.

2. To have the love of his girlfriend.

He had a compulsive idea that tied and knotted his love for his girlfriend to his love for his father. So that any sexual enjoyment—any jouissance—would automatically be equated with an imaginary attack on his father:

If I have a wish to see a woman naked, then my father will be bound to die

Because the obsessional believes that his two desires are mutually exclusive, that for him to act on the one, would be to rule out his following the other, he reasons:

> In a naïve sense it may have been possible for the man to reconcile his love for his father with his love for girlfriend, but in the young man's mind it was Impossible, because he saw his two desires as incompatible. His whole life became centred on this impossibility; he found himself endlessly repeating tasks, backwards and forwards, to and fro, and he repeatedly moved, from one mutually exclusive desire, to the other, and then back again, without understanding why, as he wrestled with his impossibility or the real.

Either I do X, which is impossible because I want Y,

or

I do Y, which is impossible because I desire X.

I can't give up X because I desire X.

I can't give up Y because I desire Y.

The obsessional is a bit like an accountant who is desperately trying to balance the books of a company that trades very rapidly; the oscillating income and expenditure, the two desires are offset against one another, pushing and pulling, dominating the obsessional's life. This is why an obsessional asks 'Am I alive or dead?' His frenetic activities make little or no difference to either of his desires overall, because he always sets one against the other. He often imagines that he is living a kind of death because he fails to complete anything, or to act fully on either of his desires.

PERVERSION OR PERE-VERSION?

Perversion is in some ways the joker in the pack of psychopathology. Perverts are usually contented with their symptom—they enjoy them so much that they rarely ask for psychoanalysis.

To understand perversion we will have to rely on another of Lacan's developments from Freud's theory, the phallus.

WHAT IS 'THE PHALLUS'? AND WHAT IS 'CASTRATION'?

The phallus is not defined as the penis, although the penis is one example of the phallus, a privileged one.

This is not
The phallus

------->

The phallus is something that has the power to move or change, apparently by itself. Examples of the phallus are motorbikes, a business that expands and contracts, women making babies, workmen building a house, a plough cutting a furrow, a penis getting small and getting big. So women can be phallic, and men can be phallic. But men and women are often phallic in different ways. It is usual to believe that someone else—the other—either has or is the phallus, which the subject wants to possess. Women often regard a man or baby as the phallus; a man typically believes that a woman possesses the phallus.

One may, simply by reference to the function of the phallus, indicate the structures that will govern the relations between the sexes. These relations will turn around a 'to be the phallus' and, on a 'to have the phallus'.

There is a rude and phallic caricature that 'a man thinks with his penis', and its counterpart that 'a woman thinks with her womb'. Both these ways of understanding sexuality are phallic, because the penis and the womb expand and contract, and so are attributed with power.

Power is represented by the phallic function, and loss of power is represented by castration. Wherever the phallus functions there is also 'castration'. Castration in this sense has nothing to do with the removal of testicles or ovaries but with a loss of power—that is, with a diminution in the phallic function. The phallus and castration are counterparts, like 'black and white' or 'good and bad'. So a psychoanalyst might say of an athlete, suffering with a heavy dose of flu and due to run an important race, that 'she is castrated'. A woman might be 'castrated' if her business fails, if her car breaks down, or if she discovers that she is not able to have the children she wanted. So the idea of a limit, as demonstrated by a rise or fall, is the phallic function.

The child is typically the phallus of the motherer; she uses the child to produce enjoyment for herself. It is this enjoyment or jouissance of the phallus, by the motherer, that is aimed at by the pervert's symptom.

The pervert making himself the instrument of the jouissance of the other

For a French pervert, sexual satisfaction took the form of masturbating while a prostitute defecated on him, saying, as the shit emerged:

There are two readings of this utterance: one, 'merde', is 'shit': another is 'mère de' which translates as 'mother of'. The shit appears in this perverse fantasy as 'the phallus of the mother'.

The jouissance of the pervert is taken up in his symptom which distinguishes the penis from the phallus.

A child's intercourse with anyone responsible for his care affords him an unending source of sexual excitement and satisfaction from his erotogenic zones. This is especially so since the person in charge of him, who after all, is as a rule, his mother, herself regarding him with feelings that are derived from her own sexual life: she strokes him, kisses him, rocks him, and quite clearly treats him as a substitute for a complete sexual object.

Lacan spoke of 'père-version', where 'père' is French for 'father', because he understood jouissance to be at the heart of perversion, and jouissance is always transgressive, somehow against a rule, as an illicit variation. Paradoxically, to take jouissance is against rules, and also, in accordance with rules; there are always rules and taboos about how we must and must not enjoy ourselves. Père-version refers to the symbolic father because the symbolic father separates the child from the motherer and so is identified with the rules of taboo and enjoyment. The rules against incest disallow the son from enjoying the mother in the same ways that the father does, and disallow the daughter from enjoying the father as the mother does.

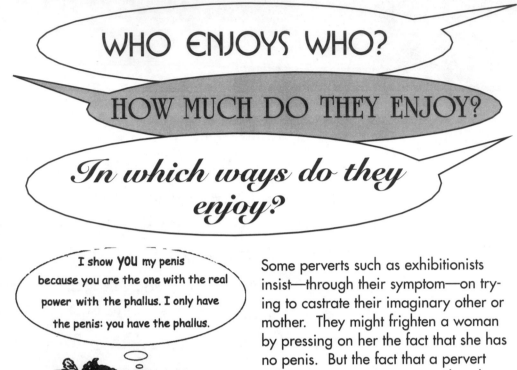

WHO ENJOYS WHO?

HOW MUCH DO THEY ENJOY?

In which ways do they enjoy?

> I show **YOU** my penis because you are the one with the real power with the phallus. I only have the penis: you have the phallus.

Some perverts such as exhibitionists insist—through their symptom—on trying to castrate their imaginary other or mother. They might frighten a woman by pressing on her the fact that she has no penis. But the fact that a pervert wants a woman to recognise that she does not have a penis demonstrates that he actually attributes the woman with a special power; he believes that she has the phallus, not the penis. The pervert uses his symptom to reestablish his belief that she has the phallus, that is to reestablish his own castration, via the m/other's castration.

All neurotics probably have some perverse traits, especially if they are men. Some women demonstrate their awareness and manipulation of this perversion in the detailed attention they give to the objects associated with their phallic power and sexuality, such as shoes, while complaining that men treat them as objects.

Now, which shoe will excite and interest men the most?

CHAPTER 8

PSYCHOSIS

Typically these hallucinations are accompanied by grandiose and persecutory ideas. Sometimes psychotics are paranoid and believe that they are being personally and uniquely addressed by the television newscaster, that aliens are monitoring and controlling their thoughts, or that they alone are responsible for the welfare of the nation. Psychotics however often have extraordinary beliefs such as 'I am Jesus Christ', or 'Aliens are following me', that lead them to make dramatic changes in their lives. We can understand these symptoms as an enormous emphasis on the big other.

P sychosis is in some ways the most dramatic and extraordinary of the four clinical structures. What sorts of things do psychotics experience and do? Psychotics caricature the popular idea of 'the mad person' and are often unable to follow a career or intimate long term relationships for some or for all of their lives. A person suffering from psychosis will often have hallucinations of voices, and be uncomfortably conscious of being looked at—remember 'the gaze' and 'the voice' as examples of the little other?

CAN A SUBJECT BE JUST 'A BIT PSYCHOTIC', OR 'A BORDERLINE CASE'?

Remember that Lacan thought your psychic structure would always be dominated by one of the four psychic structures: hysteria, obsessional neurosis, perversion, or psychosis.

Lacan thought that psychosis is like pregnancy: you have it or you don't.

You can't be a bit pregnant, and, argues Lacan, you can't be a bit psychotic, you either are or are not psychotic. This position is very different from Melanie Klein's: she thought that we are all a bit psychotic, some of us more so than others.

This Klein-Lacan debate is complicated by two facts that often make it difficult to diagnose psychosis: the first we have already met; it is the problem of the same outward behaviour often having different underlying psychic structures. So, for example, some people, who are usually called by psychiatrists 'manic depressive', may appear to have some psychotic symptoms, while others may not. There are other examples of symptoms that can mimic psychosis such as hysterics who also hear voices and sometimes believe that they are being persecuted; so the diagnosis of psychosis is not always straightforward.

The second problem in diagnosing psychosis is that some people will lead their lives, apparently as neurotics, and then suddenly have a psychotic episode. For some psychotics, symptoms are not continuous, but may appear every few months or only once or twice in their lifetime—or even never at all! They have a neurotic layer or facade that lies over their psychotic structure. So it is possible, if nothing disturbs and triggers the underlying psychotic structure, for psychotics never to show any obvious psychotic symptoms for the whole of their lives!

This situation is a bit like someone who would be allergic to penicillin if they took it, but in fact they never have taken it. We would probably still want to say—assuming we knew—that such a person 'is allergic to penicillin', or would be, because they are capable, with their structure, of generating an allergic response to penicillin.

So there is a gulf between an underlying structure of neurosis or psychosis, and the symptoms or language presented by those underlying structures. It is therefore not straightforward diagnosing a structure as psychotic or neurotic because meaning in general is not fixed, but in flux. The difference between a neurotic and a psychotic is their language. Psychotics use language—or to be more Lacanian—are **used by** language in a different way from neurotics.

There is a bit more theory on this idea in the next section before we look at a clinical case of psychosis.

The symbolic father and the 'Names of the father'

The basis of this joke is the fact that while there is nearly always a question of paternity—as to who the father is—there is hardly ever a question of maternal identity. So your knowledge of your mother's identity is relatively certain or fixed, while your knowledge of your father's identity is far less certain and so is more likely to change.

With this mixture of paternity and identity in mind Lacan conceived 'the Names-of-the-father', which, he argued, has the special function of making psychotic structure radically different from neurotic structure.

Unfortunately, there is more than the usual amount of guesswork required here, because Lacan never gave a course of seminars on the 'Names-of-the-father' as he did with many of his other ideas. To explain the 'Names-of-the-father' is not easy; we will need a detour around naming, the symbolic father, and the extraordinary work of the logician Kurt Godel, which will help to make sense of Lacan's theory.

Lacan thought that to speak—to use language—you have to be separated from your motherer. If you are not properly separated from your motherer (by the 'mother tongue') then it will show in your language. What counts as proper separation? What is it in the separation from the motherer that allows the subject to speak? Lacan's answer is 'proper names'.

Lacan argued that the function of proper names allows a separation from the motherer, which in turn allows language. Without the special function of names we would not be able to speak and understand language, argued Lacan. Because psychotics have not been properly separated by names—from their motherer—they have a different relation to language, and a different way of speaking from neurotics.

To make sense of this we should review Lacan's concept: 'the symbolic father'. A kind of separation of the child from the motherer is carried out by the symbolic father, which could be the motherer's work, lover or siblings. But this symbolic father is not enough for proper and permanent separation that would prevent psychosis, because the identity of the symbolic father often changes, it is not fixed. So the separation of the child from the motherer would also vary as the identity of the separator—of the symbolic father—varied. What is required to prevent psychosis is a separation that is fixed and permanent. This permanence is a property of proper names, of the Names-of-the-father.

For neurotics the Names-of-the-father are properly repressed and lie forever in the unconscious. But in psychosis the Names-of-the-father have not been properly repressed. To compensate for this lack of repression, psychotics introduce new identities into their lives that will then work to provide new repressions, that would otherwise be absent for them. These new repressions prop up their psychic structure and allow them to continue using language. What form do these new repressions take?

Often psychotics will speak about their being persecuted or controlled by aliens, of seeking asylum in a foreign country, or of changing gender.

In these cases there is the introduction of a new and conspicuous repressive identity that has the function of holding together language for them. These new and conscious entities have the function for psychotics that the Names-of-the-father have in the unconscious for neurotics.

HOW DOES THIS 'HOLDING TOGETHER' OF LANGUAGE BY THE PROPER NAME WORK?

We will look at two differences and a shocking revolution in mathematics and logic to help us make two distinctions: that between proper names and other words, and the difference between the symbolic father and the Names-of-the-father.

Let's distinguish the Names-of-the-father from Lacan's related idea, the symbolic father, who we met in chapter four. The symbolic father is any agency separating the child from the motherer. To find out how this Names-of-the-Father idea is different from the 'symbolic father' we should first look at some differences between proper nouns like 'Fred', 'Smith' and other types of word such as 'table', 'house', 'white' and 'gay'.

Take 'gay': it used to mean 'jolly, happy', but today it usually means 'homosexual', or 'blue' which at one time meant only a specific colour but now also refers to a mood of melancholy. But a proper name like 'Fred Smith' doesn't change its meaning in the same way as a word like 'blue' or 'gay': 'Fred Smith' will always refer to the particular person or persons called 'Fred Smith', whatever happens to the English language over time. Proper names are forever glued to whatever they originally referred to. Lacan argues that there is a fixity about proper names that is absent in the other words in our language whose meanings shift. One type of fixed meaning are called 'axioms' or rules.

Now we have a digression to make, to the philosophy of mathematics and logic, to look at what Gödel had to say about how meaning is and is not fixed with rules, before we return to language and psychosis.

KURT GODEL'S REVOLUTIONARY INCOMPLETENESS THEOREM

Kurt Gödel (1906-1978) was a logician and philosopher who is famous for having produced a logical proof about elementary number theory. He proved that there are rules that are true yet unprovable!

Before Gödel's revolutionary work in 1931, it was taken for granted by all mathematicians that what was true could always be proved, and that everything would eventually become clear and proven, in just the same way that it was taken for granted after Newton's discoveries, that we would fully understand all the workings of the world. But, as with Heisenberg's work —which overthrew Newton's tidy scheme— Gödel discovered a very surprising impossibility, a logically necessary impossibility, something that cannot be avoided. He destroyed the naïve and ideal conception of mathematics as 'the true and provable'.

Put simply, Gödel proved that if you want to make a complete list of all the rules for making numbers, like a kind of grammar of numbers, then there are only two possibilities:

 **Either**

the list of rules will be incomplete, that is there will be some rules missing — which is a problem if you want a complete list.

Or

there will be some inconsistency, that is there will be contradictions between some of the rules. Obviously if two rules contradict one another, it follows that they can't both be true; one of them must be false. This is a problem because inconsistency is something that mathematicians and logicians avoid like the plague. It guarantees for them that there is something fatally wrong.

Very famous mathematician

JOHN VON NEUMANN

These paired mutual exclusivities of Gödel, of inconsistency and incompleteness are reminiscent of Heisenberg's electron, where you can either find out the electron's speed, or its position, but you can't find out both.

"Gödel was the first man to demonstrate that certain mathematical theorems can **neither be proved nor disproved with the accepted, rigorous methods of mathematics.** In other words **he demonstrated the existence of undecidable mathematical propositions.** He proved furthermore that a very important specific proposition belonged to this class of undecidable problems: The question: **'is mathematics free of inner contradictions'?** The result is remarkable in its quasi-paradoxical 'self denial': **It will never be possible to acquire with mathematical means the certainty that mathematics does not contain contradictions.** It must be emphasized that the important point is, that **this is not a philosophical principle** or a plausible intellectual attitude, but the result of a rigorous mathematical proof."

117

So Gödel proved that **any** system that is more complicated than counting must be either inconsistent (contradicts itself) or incomplete. And
let's face it, people can count and much more besides —we are much
more complex than counting machines— so people must be 'either
incomplete or inconsistent'. How does this forced choice between
inconsistency and incompleteness relate to Lacan's theory of psychosis?

Put roughly, Lacan's hypothesis about psychosis goes like this: for adults
the generative base —that is the set of rules that produces language—
is partially fixed. The generative base is like a grammar that produces
all the different kinds of language and symptoms that each of us have.
When we can use a language properly we can make a potentially infinite number of sentences, with every one of them grammatically correct,
if we are not drunk or tired.

The underlying rules for generating all this extraordinary variety gradually become more fixed as children learn language. But it is probably
true to say that there is a partially different set of rules for each person
who speaks the same language. This would explain why we sometimes
argue about the meanings of words.

When the fixed rules are laid down, as if they are written in stone,
some rules can be fixed that are not consistent with each other, so that
the rules contradict each other. For most people, for neurotics and perverts, the rules are not generally inconsistent but incomplete, that is,
there are rules missing.

It is not for us
to **complete** the work
but neither may we
desist from it

But for psychotics, the fundamental rules are contradictory; they have some fixed rules that are in conflict. So every pervert and neurotic lives his life with his own unique and changing incompleteness. But for the psychotic there are fixed rules that contradict one another, producing their very distressing symptoms of paranoia and hallucinations.

Where do the contradictory rules of psychotics come from? From the symbolic father, and from the Names-of-the-Father as we will see. But remember the relation that words like 'table' and 'mean' have in relation to proper names like 'Fred Smith'? The fixity of proper names and the flux of adjectives and nouns are mutually supportive, and mutually dependent. They feed off one another. So it is with the symbolic father and with the Names—of—the—Father. The symbolic father is a thing in flux that changes because what separates the child from its motherer can change, but the Names-of-the Father are fixed, and once written can never be erased.

The fixity of proper names and the flux of common nouns and adjectives seem to be properties that rely mutually on one another. So proper names depend on the other bits of language, and the other bits of language depend on proper names.

fixed meanings: names

variable meanings: nouns, verbs...

For example, the symbolic father might be the biological father to start with, and then become a step-father, or sibling, and later be the motherer's work.

But, while the identity of the symbolic father has been in flux, certain proper names have had their reference fixed. Perhaps with 'Simon', as the name of the biological father, 'Fred', as the name of the step father and 'Safeway', where the motherer works. So the child will have fixed some aspects of the symbolic father as proper names. It is these fixed rules that are the Names-of-the-Father.

The symbolic father may be more than 'one thing', such as 'the biological father', 'the stepfather', and 'the motherer's work'. But whatever bits make it up, the separation of motherer and child is seen by the child as the motherer's desire for someone other than itself. The aspects of the symbolic father that remain in flux are not the Names-of-the-Father.

Those aspects of the symbolic father that become fixed, as the rules of grammar, are the Names-of-the-Father.

Take the jobs of weaving and being a blacksmith. The meaning of 'weaving' is not precisely fixed; it might refer to weaving baskets, cloth or magic spells. Now think of the times when people were called after their occupations: Such as 'Simon Blacksmith' or 'Helen Weaver'. Here you can see how nouns became proper names. In their passage to proper namehood, the nouns with variable meaning have come to have their meaning fixed; 'Simon Blacksmith' will always refer to a particular individual whatever 'Blacksmith' comes to mean as a noun, even thousands of years after he has died.

How does this help
explain psychosis?

Lacan said that in psychosis:

There is a `foreclosure of
the Names-of-the-father'

What did he mean?

What does 'foreclosure' mean?
Foreclosure is a kind of exclusion which
occurs following the breaking of a contract. For instance when a mortgage
lender forcloses on your mortgage, he
excludes you from your home because
you have failed to keep to the rules of
your side of the contract with him.

All of us, psychotics and neurotics, have had a contract with the Names-
of-the-father. The terms of the contract are: as long as you do not speak
the Names-of-the-father you will be permitted to live in the house of
ordinary neurotic language. So, neurotics maintain their contracts with
the Names-of-the-father while psychotics cannot.

How does the psychotic break his contract? He cannot keep the Names-
of-the-father repressed and unspoken.

Perhaps this is why Jews are
forbidden -on pain of death- to
properly pronounce God's
name?

Why? Because he has not been rigidly and properly separated from his motherer, so the rules of language and meaning are not properly fixed for psychotics. So when psychotics speak they always have some meanings that are far too fixed, and some that are far too loose, because the rules do not accord with the contract that binds neurotics. So when a psychotic was told that a messy room looked like a bomb had gone off in it, he jumped in fright, as if a bomb had literally gone off.

So if you have a mortgage on a house, and say 'No, I can't pay the lender', the lender will 'foreclose on the mortgage'. He will repossess your house and kick you out of it. Then the name of your lender will ring in your ears, as he who has separated you from your cosy home. In psychosis there is a price that the psychotic has not paid, and cannot pay. That price is the proper separation from the motherer, as marked out by the Names-of-the-father. Because the psychotic has not paid the price of separation from the motherer, language does not function for the psychotic as it does for the neurotic.

The evil XZY BANK have foreclosed on the mortgage and evicted me. I am seperated from my home now, but I will get another one

HOME SWEET HOME

From a clinical point of view many psychotics are taken up in an extraordinary way with identity and with names. They may insist that they have been reincarnated and demand to be called by a different name, or wish to change their nationality, have sex change operations, or claim that a spell has been put on them that is changing their gender, identity and sexual orientation.

There is a clinical history often seen in cases of psychosis that involves either an absent and hence inconsistent symbolic father, or a very harsh or powerful symbolic father. We will see that these two sorts of symbolic fathers can amount to the same thing.

123

THE ROLE OF AN ABSENT SYMBOLIC FATHER IN PSYCHOSIS

In the case of an absent symbolic father, the child first establishes that the motherer must have had a desire for someone other than himself, at least for a symbolic father whose sperm made him. That is, the mother desired someone who was not the child.

Then the child finds that the symbolic father is not present; he establishes in his own mind that the motherer does not desire anyone else, she does not desire the symbolic father. **So the symbolic father was present and then absent;** hence the inconsistency, or contradiction, and the accord with Gödel's work.

Now it is time to relate Lacan's theory to a clinical case:

It is not unusual for psychotics to have a history like that of a young man whose father left the family home when he was two years old. From that time until he was ten he slept in his mother's bed, and did not know of any interest his mother had in any lover who had taken his absent father's place. When he was seventeen he was persecuted by voices telling him that he was gay, and imagined that UFOs were communicating with him. These complaints completely dominated his life.

The inconsistency here is the **presence** and **absence** of the symbolic father, who, in this case also happened to be the biological father—not only the physical absence but also the symbolic absence; for the son had taken his father's place in the matrimonial bed. Lacan's hypothesis would probably be that this psychotic man had a pair of inconsistent rules, possibly along the following lines:

1. Up to age two, while there was someone —the symbolic father— separating him from his mother, he could say:

2. After his second birthday, when he started sleeping with his mother, there was no symbolic father separating him from his mother:

There is someone my mother desires who IS NOT me.

There is no one my mother desires who is not me; I am the only person she desires, because THERE IS NO ONE to separate us.

With neurotics and perverts there is a triangular relation between a child, its motherer and the symbolic father. This triangular relation, with three rather than two people, which is also known as 'The Oedipus relation', ensures that the child is separated from its motherer, preventing the inconsistency described above from arising.

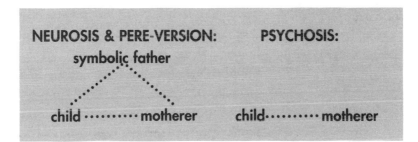

NEUROSIS & PERE-VERSION:
symbolic father

child ········· motherer

PSYCHOSIS:

child········· motherer

For psychotics there is a problem identifying the motherer's desire for anyone other than themselves. They have failed to find anyone else whom the motherer desires. This often produces paranoia: grandiosity and ideas of persecution. Imagine, if you have someone who is enormously important in your life — your motherer— and you fail to find her desire for anyone besides yourself? You would be bound to see yourself as overly important; your world being totally dominated by one person and their desire for you.

In order to escape this vision of your life as totally dominated by this one person's exclusive desire FOR YOU, you have a solution:

PERSECUTION!

The idea of persecution introduces an other who takes up a position separating the subject from the motherer. In the case of the young man who had slept in his mother's bed since he was two, we can see his thorough identification with his mother, that is, his lack of separation from her. He complained that he was persecuted by images of sex with men, and protested 'I am not homosexual'; and it was the place of a man that he took in his mother's bed.

But if the psychotic young man was to become a practising homosexual, then an important difference would become established: a distinction would be drawn between the young man and his mother, and they would then have become separate, because there would be a third person between them, because in fantasy the homosexual lover would be someone who both desired the young man, and was desired by the mother, so breaking the child-motherer duo.

For the young man, his feared object of love appears to be the same as his mother's object of love, a man. This shared object of love would contrive the third element of the triangular or Oedipal relation that neurotics have, but too late to prevent psychosis.

In this case, the psychotic fantasies of sex with a third person, a man, caused torment, but seemed also to have had the function of preventing a more devastating breakdown. The fantasy of the third person has the effect of preventing the inconsistency in the rules becoming apparent, by insisting —through paranoia— that **there is someone** who **does** separate the subject from the motherer.

As Lacan observed, the symptom is always a solution to a problem.

THE ROLE OF AN OVERBEARING SYMBOLIC FATHER IN PSYCHOSIS

Little Daniel Schreber was subjected to these machines by his overbearing father and grew up to become psychotic, and was studied by Freud

Now it is time to explain how an overbearing, powerful and highly repressive symbolic father, such as a leader, can be equivalent to an absent symbolic father. Such a man is likely to be 'too much' for his children. He may, by being 'too strong' and highly repressive, increase the chance of having children who grow up to become psychotic. How can we explain this? By the fact that the father cannot possibly be present all the time. So that when he is absent, his absence is felt far more, again producing an inconsistency.

REPRESSION AND EXPRESSION IN AND OUT OF PSYCHOSIS

The idea of the absence or harshness of the symbolic father being important in psychosis is closely connected to Freud's and Lacan's theory of repression as learning. If we are to have an even chance of getting a mix of hysteria, obsessionality, and perversion, we should have an even amount of repression throughout our lives, without any peaks or troughs. So, in this unrealistic thought experiment there would be no traumas and no dramatic episodes of the sort that we have all experienced, just a thoroughly homogenous, bland, tame life.

What actually happens is that because repression varies, because we learn different things with different intensities, we each end up with one of the four different psychic structures: hysteria, obsessional neurosis, perversion or psychosis.

Psychotics, however have a kind of freedom, despite and because of their terrible symptoms. They can question in a more radical way than the rest of us, taking issue with things that most of us take for granted. Neurotics and perverts have more that is rigidly fixed, that cannot be questioned.

Perhaps this is one reason that explains why psychosis is associated with creativity and genius, and some of the greatest talents, including van Gogh, Cantor, Gödel and Joyce seem to have been psychotic.

CHAPTER 9

Feminine Sexuality

WHAT DOES IT MEAN TO BE A WOMAN?

What does a woman want?

Throughout history people have knocked their heads against the riddle of the nature of femininity

To get clearer about what it means to be a woman — for Lacan— we should start with something simpler; what it means to be a man, and the role of the phallus. Understanding the phallus is central to Lacan's theory of feminine sexuality. Lacan thought that there are two kinds of sexuality: phallic and non-phallic. Masculine sexuality is phallic, whilst the sexuality of women is both phallic and non-phallic or 'feminine'.

So women have something that men do not. But there is also a special category of those who have non-phallic sexuality —who can either be men or women— who can help explain the mystery of feminine sexuality:

mystics.

	MEN	WOMEN	MYSTICS (of whatever gender)
PHALLIC SEXUALITY	YES	YES	YES
NON-PHALLIC OR FEMININE SEXUALITY	NO	YES	YES

The mystical literature of many religions often refers to a blissful and ecstatic union of the mystic with God. This statue of Saint Theresa shows her in a state of sexual ecstasy, as a religious mystic, who clearly has jouissance in her relation with God:

On my mystical union with Christ: In Christ's hands I saw a long golden spear, he seemed to pierce my heart several times so that it penetrated to my entrails. When he drew it out, he left me afire with a continual love of God. It is not bodily pain, but spiritual, though the body has a great share in it. The pain was so great that I screamed aloud; but simultaneously I felt such infinite sweetness that I wished it to last eternally. It was not bodily but psychic pain, although it affected to a certain extent also the body. It was the sweetest caressing of the soul by God.

What might the jouissance of mystics, of either gender, have in common with feminine jouissance?

I don't understand women

The ways of God cannot be understood

What mystics have in common with women is a special relationship to the infinite

THE INFINITE

What is the infinite? 'Infinity' is not 'a number' but a special kind of counting that doesn't stop. It is, without limit. Women can produce feminine jouissance without limit because they are outside the usual rules that govern and limit phallic jouissance. Part of the usual definition of God is that he is infinite, that is without limit.

How does this help explain feminine jouissance and its relation to phallic jouissance?

The phallic is about the measurable, the observable, and that which moves and has power. Any person alive must have some interest in such things. But it seems that those of us who are masculine —at least those who are not mystics— lead their sexual lives and gain their jouissance exclusively from the phallic function. But women are not usually in this position: they do get jouissance from the phallus, but also from this other source, non-phallic or feminine jouissance. Women have phallic jouissance and feminine jouissance too.

131

WHAT CAN BE SAID ABOUT FEMININE JOUISSANCE?

Not very much, because it is not measurable **because** of its relationship to the infinite. Feminine jouissance is the stuff of feminine mystery and of mysticism. We can theorise around it, and look at feminine or non-phallic jouissance in its context, but it will always be impossible to study non-phallic jouissance directly. Phallic jouissance can be studied directly, but non-phallic jouissance or feminine jouissance is like a box that we know exists, but that cannot be opened.

`The Woman' does not exist

This means that there is an aspect of feminine sexuality that cannot be comprehended. It is for this reason that Lacan said that:

Of course, Lacan did not mean that individual women do not exist, but that it is not possible to say specifically —with a definition— what 'The Woman' is.

—Examples are one thing, definitions another—

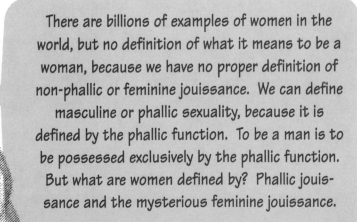

There are billions of examples of women in the world, but no definition of what it means to be a woman, because we have no proper definition of non-phallic or feminine jouissance. We can define masculine or phallic sexuality, because it is defined by the phallic function. To be a man is to be possessed exclusively by the phallic function. But what are women defined by? Phallic jouissance and the mysterious feminine jouissance.

MORE ABOUT FEMININE JOUISSANCE

But perhaps it is possible to say a little more about what we can't say much about. The phallus must rise and fall, so it has limits or boundaries, but feminine jouissance is like the infinite. Infinity, some people argue, is not actually a number, a specific amount or quantity, but rather a process of counting that fails to end, it continues, on and on... without end, without a limit: feminine jouissance is unbounded, not confined like phallic jouissance.

It is possible to construct a special mathematics around the infinite, and the 'transinfinite' as Cantor did, although it still leaves much unclear, and we can't go into that here.

But what is clear is that the history of sexuality is the history of conflict and incompatibilty, as men and women have struggled to enjoy and suffer their differences.

Men typically complain that they do not get what they want from women, nor do they understand them; women complain that they do not get what they want from men, and that they do understand men!

Because there is this mysterious feminine jouissance that men cannot access, but only observe at a distance, there will always be a mystery and incompatiblity in the attempts of men and women to relate. An explanation for this was provided by Plato's myth in which men and women originated from a single monstrous animal with eight limbs. It was split in two, as man and woman, and ever since men and women have spent much of the energy running around trying to find their other half. When they think they have found it, they try to make one together. This 'making one' is the phallic function, the idea of 'making a whole', without division, healing the suffering. And in popular culture too there is the ideal and myth that the only way for men and women to be is heterosexual.

Man cannot aim at being whole; the 'total personality' is another of the deviant premises of modern psychotherapy.

Lacan's formula of sexuation —his account of phallic and feminine jouissance— insists on the conclusion that men and women are fundamentally incompatible, or as Lacan said:

There is no such thing as a sexual relationship

THE LACK OF SEXUAL RAPPORT

Of course, Lacan did not mean that people do not have genital intercourse, but that because men and women are not the same sort of thing, because they are not both just phallic, they cannot 'relate'. If men and women were somehow equivalent to 'positive and negative', 'light and dark' or any two ends of the same continuum, then men and women could relate. But if you put a man and a woman together you don't get 'zero'. They don't 'balance out' or become 'neutral'. That is because men and women are, in important part, fundamentally different. Men, excluding the odd mystic, are totally defined by the phallic function, but women are not totally defined by the phallic function. Hence there are problems in the relations of men and women. There is no 'sexual relationship' because the difference between men and women is not on the same level or of the same type. Certainly men and women can and do have phallic relations together, but that is quite different from a relation between the phallic, or the limited and observable, and the unlimited, unbounded, feminine jouissance.

You might be able, eventually, to have a relationship with someone from another country with whom you do not share a language, by gradually learning to speak a common language. But with men and women there can be no comprehensively shared language, because there is no translation between phallic and feminine jouissance; one is in a radically different category from the other.

Homosexual relationships might appear to be a neat solution to this incompatibility problem between the genders, but they are not. In every attempt to establish sexual rapport there is always an attempt to return to the lack of rapport and built in conflict between the motherer, the symbolic father and the subject.

$$\text{man} + \text{man} = \text{non rapport}$$
$$\text{woman} + \text{woman} = \text{non rapport}$$
$$\text{woman} + \text{man} = \text{non rapport}$$

It is a common and ordinary belief that the right kind of love or sexual relation will solve all or most problems and make life easy. But how do men and women typically go about pairing up?

Women often invest a lot of resources into producing a particular type of image that is designed to be consumed by men and to captivate them, and then complain that men are only interested in what they look like; men complain that women demand too much commitment, but will often lie or mislead women as to how committed they are to the woman.

I must be attracted to her; I've had sex with her. But she's a slut for having had sex with me

I must love him; I slept with him. He must love me, he had sex with me

Many women positively idealise the man they have sex with, while many men do the opposite: they are only able to find a woman attractive if they are able to think of her as a whore, or as someone who is interested only in sex.

In fantasy, a woman's object is often one ideal

IDEALIZATION

man, while a man wants an infinitude of worthless women. These are standard caricatures of men and women, but in reality an individual man will often want love, and a women might want 'straightforward sex'; but whatever we want, we each have to come to terms with the caricatures of sexual identity, and to find our own position in relation to them.

How does Lacan think the incompatibility between men and women arises? Here is a more detailed explanation:

The newly born infant starts with the main issue being his needs, the management of his pain and pleasure. The motherer is the baby's sensation manager, controlling his pain and pleasure like a benevolent torturer; she increasingly delays gratification, causing suffering to the baby, while she feeds him words. The helpless baby soon learns that in order to get his needs addressed, he has to learn what the motherer wants. How does the baby find out what mother wants? By learning to speak, that is, by ingesting the mother's signifiers, the mother tongue.

So there is a constant shifting of the deal between the motherer and baby.

It starts off with the motherer gratifying the baby's needs as soon as they arise, but increasingly, as baby ages, the motherer changes the deal: baby gets more and more words, and less and less management of his needs, until, as adults —we live to an extraordinary degree— in the symbolic world of language.

The baby is a phallus for the motherer, a way of enjoying, and the child knows this. Motherers are usually aware to some degree that they get a sexual enjoyment from their baby. Some mothers even have orgasms while breast feeding. So the motherer gets sexual enjoyment or jouissance, and the baby gets pain. This isn't the whole story of course, but is an important and much neglected part of the problem of gender and sexual identity.

The baby suffered pain, and then the extraordinary substitution of language for pleasure, through his motherer feeding him words. The baby has —as the foundation of his relation with his motherer— his shocking frustration, the pain and pleasure, and the language that replaced food, fed to him by his motherer.

When the child has language, he usually discovers that he is not the only one whom the motherer desires; the child has to share the motherer with another child, or with the motherer's lover or with her work. That is, he has to live with the symbolic father, with the motherer's desire for some other, or be psychotic.

You can see that there are two major shifts for the baby, two broken deals or incompatibilities, where he doesn't get what he wants:

1. He wants pleasure or no pain, but instead gets language and pain.
2. He wants full access to motherer, but gets limited access.

The child's whole relation to the motherer is necessarily founded on not getting what it wants, on the establishment of an incompatibility or lack of rapport. Adult sexuality is based on this lack of rapport between the motherer and the child. The motherer-child relation is the prototype for all adult sexual relations.

If there were perfect rapport between the child and motherer, with the child having every need instantly gratified, then the child would never learn to speak and would never be forced to enter the world of language with its variable meanings and confusing sexuality.

...a child sucking at his mother's breast has become the prototype of every relation of love

It is my belief that, however strange it may sound, we must reckon with possibility that something in the nature of the sexual drive itself is unfavourable to the realization of complete satisfaction

One gets the impression that a man's love and a woman's are a phase apart psychologically

CHAPTER 10

TIME AND TOPOLOGY

What is time? Time is THE measure of change. You can only tell that time has passed because something has changed, even if it is only the position of clock hands. What has this got to do with psychoanalysis?

Psychoanalysis is a theory of psychic change, of the ways in which people change, so it is not surprising that psycho-analysis has something to say about the ways in which those changes are perceived and conceived.

'Time' is a complicated topic, about which Lacan had some interesting things to say, although, as with so many other issues, he changed his mind, with time. We won't be con-cerned here about the metaphysical questions of time, such as are raised by Einstein's and Hawking's theories, but about the psy-chological ones. It may turn out in the end that the two are connected, but we won't worry about that.

To take the idea of conception, and of birth, it is commonly thought that a person's identity only begins to become established after their birth. But long before a baby is born or even conceived his parents already have a set of demands and desires, against which the child will have to develop his own demand and desire. Perhaps the parents will demand that their baby be 'like his daddy', or 'heterosexual', French, or an accountant.

Language and its structures exist prior to the moment at which each subject at a certain point in his mental development makes his entry into it

Congratulations, you have a fine homosexual

It must be remarked that the lateness of dentition and of walking, a lateness correlative for the majority of bodily equipment and functions, indicates in the infant a total vital impotence which lasts through the first two years.

Freud and Lacan argued that all human infants are born 'prematurely'. By this they mean that if you compare a human aged two, with a dog, horse, or lizard aged two, the human is the most inept and the least independent. The baby has probably only just learnt to stumble about and can't feed or care for itself. In all the animal kingdom human babies are the most helpless for the longest. Why? It is essential that we endure a lengthy dependency in order that we learn language, the mother tongue.

To check on this ask yourself: With which chimp below do you identify more closely?

Almost everyone seems to prefer the baby chimp on the left over the adult chimp. This similarity between baby chimps and human adults led one writer to say that what is essential in mankind as an organism is:

> ...the slow progress of his life's course. This slow tempo is the result of a retardation' and '...man, in his bodily development, is a primate foetus that has become sexually mature.... . What is a transitional stage in the ... [individual development] of other primates has become a terminal stage in man' ...[M]an is a primate foetus that has become sexually mature'.

So there is an important sense in which people are retarded chim panzees. In this version of 'The Hare and the Tortoise' it is our being retarded or slow that has given each of us the time to become dominated by language, by signifiers. Our progress, as chimps, has been interrupted, allowing the language of variable meanings to take the place of the fixed meanings of instinct (remember that 'red' always means 'do a mating dance' for sticklebacks).

This idea of 'interruption' and of 'fixed meaning' is taken up with Lacan's famous invention, 'the variable length session'. To understand this you should appreciate that before Lacan psychoanalytic sessions lasted a fixed fifty minutes. During fixed length sessions clients often talk about the weather and all sorts of things distant from their problems until the last few minutes when they discuss more important matters, but with the 'protection' of knowing that they can escape close scrutiny of their more painful issues, because they will be saved by the end of the session. Why have sessions that last fifty minutes? What is so important about fifty minutes?

Just about the only things in life that take exactly fifty minutes are school lessons and fixed length psychoanalytic sessions.

Almost all human activities are not of fixed chronological length: making love, making meals and arguments are all of variable duration.

Lacan's radical practice involved ending a session at the point when an important question or ambiguity had been made clear in the client's speech. This might take fifteen minutes, twenty five minutes or an hour. Choosing to end on a question means that everything a client says must be listened to carefully by the analyst and the client, and that the client will leave the session with some important loose ends to consider and do some homework on. Ending a session on a client's question also emphasizes an important truth: the analyst really does not have the answers to his client's questions, only the client might possess those through reflecting on their own questions. Reflecting on a question or ambiguity involves looking at different meanings rather than the fixed meanings that clients typically complain about.

So Lacan argued that meaning is something that we attribute afterwards. We use meaning, or are used by meaning —especially in dreams, symptoms and the slips of the tongue— and we often come to understand it only retrospectively. Lacan argued that because the subject is divided by language and word meaning, analysts should use time as a variable in sessions, not as something fixed, so the client can renegotiate his relation to meaning, with what it means to be a particular subject.

In Lacan's theory, 'the subject is divided'.

By this he means that each of us is a collection of conflicts, always being pulled in different directions.

To make things easier we all try to hide our conflicts. One technique that people use for hiding their conflicts is to try and make things 'whole' by making jouissance. A popular way of trying to make yourself whole is by joining someone else —another divided subject— and having sex. But orgasm saves the subject from division for no more than a few seconds at the most, in the loss of consciousness at orgasm.

Remember that the jouissance of orgasm is not different from the jouissance of the symptom. So one way to focus on a subject's division, and on the form that his pathology takes, is to end a session at a symptomatic point which elucidates the covering up of their subjective division. This can help the client recognise their conflicts and suffering, as well as the enjoyment or jouissance they take in their symptoms as 'solutions'.

Because the primary function of the ego is to paper over conflict and difficulty, ending a session on a point of difference, a conflict, question or dilemma, is a way of avoiding working with the ego, and colluding with it.

Recall some of the most memorable events in your life.

Generally it is the points of radical difference and change that are the most memorable. Interruptions are conspicuous points of arrest in the perceived flow of time. Lacan had noticed that if you want something a lot, it takes ages before you get it, and if you don't want something, it happens all too quickly. He was talking about a kind of 'subjective time', which is the subject's perception of the passage of time. This subjective time is not the same as the passing of time indicated on a clock, which is also known as 'chronological time'. Clock time goes on ticking away, and it provides a reference, something with which we can compare subjective time. Clock time is associated with the big other, the other of language, and subjective time with the little other, the little object of desire. So the rate of subjective time has a lot to do with how much has been completed, in relation to our needs, demands and desires.

Are we nearly there?

Are we nearly there?

Time and Meaning

What has time got to do with meaning? We saw how the meaning of being a chimpanzee changed enormously because there was a specific change of timing, an interruption, allowing the evolution of humans as a radically different kind of chimpanzee. Being a particular kind of retarded chimpanzee means being a human. But if you were an alien biologist, studying life on earth, you would probably be surprised by the huge differences between the ways that chimps and people live, given that the difference between them appears to be mostly due to a difference of timing that retarded bodily development, but allowed sexual maturity.

It is differences of timing that allow signifiers to have variable meanings. Meanings that change, depending on their context. So it is nearly always necessary to wait for some time after a word has first been used, in order to begin to understand the meaning, to grasp the context. Here is an example:

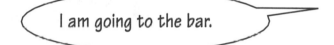

I am going to the bar.

Does this mean that the speaker is going to have a drink, or that he has reached the point in his legal training where he is to become a barrister?

Only on waiting might you find out the answer to these or other questions.

Perhaps the speaker, if listened to for just a moment longer would have been heard to say:

I am going to the barn.

If you listened longer still you might have discovered that 'I am going to the barn' was actually used as a password, and that it had a wholly different meaning from the one you had understood earlier.

I'm going to stop your clock -that is the meaning of my existence- what is the meaning of yours?

Jokes are a better example of this phenomenon; jokes are not understood until the punchline. The punchline has the effect of giving meaning to the whole of the joke. So meaning operates retrospectively, that is, with the passage of time.

LIFE
DEATH

EXPRESSION
REPRESSION

But it is not only jokes that get their meaning retrospectively. All the words that have ever been spoken or written have their meanings changed continually. You can see this for instance in the work of scientists, where the word 'mass', for example takes on a new meaning in Einstein's theory, which came after Newton's theory. The work of historians is also to find new meanings in old words.

Psychoanalysis aims at helping clients find meanings in their words and symptoms. Typically clients repeat certain words and phrases that have special hidden importance for them. It can take years of psychoanalysis to explore the shifting meanings of these special phrases. So every psychoanalytic session is a discovering of new meanings in old words.

Psychoanalysis is like an archaeological investigation of an ancient site with many layers, each one overlaid by a different but related culture, that took over the one before it.

What is topology and why was Lacan interested in it?

One of the best ways to understand 'psychic archaeology' is with a discipline from mathematics called 'topology'.

Freud had discovered that if you want to understand the mind, ordinary three dimensional space is not enough:

Now let us, by a flight of imagination, suppose that Rome is not a human habitation but a psychical entity with a similarly long and copious past... There is no point in spinning our phantasy any further, for it leads to things that are unimaginable and even absurd. ...The same space cannot have two different contents. Our attempt seems to be an idle game. It has only one justification. It shows us how far we are from mastering the characteristics of mental life by representing them in pictorial terms.

'Time and space' come as a package, together; as time is the measure of change, so space is the place of change. 'Topology' is concerned with time and space and is also known as 'rubber sheet geometry', because angle and distance are not variables in topology; they do not exist. So, for example, a car tire and a needle are identical topologically because in topology you could deform a needle —as if it were elastic— so that it took the form of a tyre, or vice versa, because both objects have a hole in them, and topology assumes all objects and space to be rubbery, or distortable.

Topology deals with a kind of space that is more fundamental than our ordinary everyday three dimensional space. Of course we ordinarily see the world as three dimensional, but many processes in psychoanalysis (and physics and mathematics) can only be understood with a more general topological scheme of elastic time and space. The kind it seems each of us has in our minds; time and distance are famously elastic from the position of the subject's desire. Typically, if you want something, it takes a long time to happen; and if you don't want it, it happens much too soon. Topology sometimes breaks fleetingly through the façade of our everyday three dimensional geometry, twisting and distorting in dreams, hallucinations and fantasies of time and distance.

Topology is especially important in understanding language and its role in psychoanalysis because it doesn't make much sense to speak of 'the distance between words'. Words are connected to each other, but the connections do not seem to have any length. This topological view, with the disappearance of the ordinary understanding of distance, is what is meant by 'the shrinking world' or the 'global village', in the flow of signifiers in telecommunications. In a telephone conversation between someone in England and someone in Australia —as far apart as possible— there is no distance between their signifiers.

Because 'the signifier represents the subject for another signifier', the absence of distance between signifiers implies a lack of distance between subjects. This means that each subject is spread, like an elastic net or fluid around the global language community, and distributed amongst the universe of all those who are subject to signifiers.

Instructions on how to make your mind up

OR

Make your own model of the mind

Here is a topological object you can make yourself.
IYou will need a strip of paper, approximately 1 inch
wide x 11 inches high, a pair of scissors and a piece of
sticky tape about two inches long (five centimetres).

1. Check that the strip has two sides!

2. Take hold of one end of the strip with the thumb
    and forefinger of one hand.

3. Take hold of the other end of the strip, with the
    thumb and forefinger of your other hand, and
    make a 180° twist with one end.

4. Now touch the two ends of the strip together and
    tape them, all the way around the edges.

You now own a Mobius band.

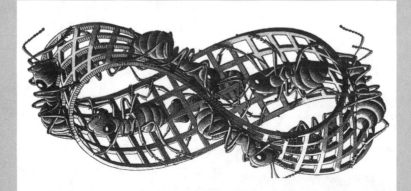

The Mobius band is special because it used to be an ordinary piece of paper with two sides but now it has only one side! You can prove it has only one side by drawing a continuous line down the middle of it. You will soon return to the point you started drawing the line from, proving therefore that the band must have only one side, because you haven't turned it over!

What has the Mobius band got to do with psychoanalysis? The Mobius band is a topological model or structure of the way that some things work in the mind. Why? Because, like topology, the band disregards distance; it doesn't matter how far you go along it, you will always return to the point at which you started.

The subject knows that to want to 'not desire', has in itself something as irrefutable as that Moebius strip that has no underside, that is to say, that in following it, one will come back mathematically to the surface that is supposed to be its other side.

So the Mobius band is for Lacan, a model of the real, of that which returns. One important kind of return of the real is the return of the repressed.

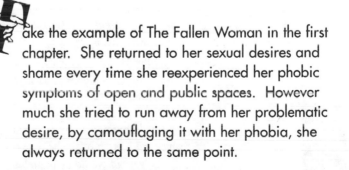

Take the example of The Fallen Woman in the first chapter. She returned to her sexual desires and shame every time she reexperienced her phobic symptoms of open and public spaces. However much she tried to run away from her problematic desire, by camouflaging it with her phobia, she always returned to the same point.

CHAPTER 11

WHAT'S THE GOOD OF PSYCHOANALYSIS?

If you are analysed you will come to revalue and review what 'good' and 'bad' mean for you. But good or bad are the stuff of ethics, along with the questions and answers as to what we 'ought to do'. Lacan argued that ethical considerations can only be properly made after desire has been identified. Before you can place a value on things, or decide what is good or bad you first have to know your desire. So the purpose of analysis is the analysis of purpose. You have to know what your desires are before you can begin to get clear about your values. A version of this idea is used in the courts of law where the question of the accused's desire is often the most important issue for a judge or jury:

Members of the jury, the question you have to answer is: When the defendant stabbed this man in the neck with a pair of scissors, what was his desire? If the accused's desire was murderous, then he would be guilty of murder. But, if his desire was of a different type, such as the desire to cut and style the man's hair, and he happened to be pushed in an accident, which led him to stab the man's neck, then the verdict would be manslaughter...

So ethical issues can only be decided after the main issues of desire have been clarified. The question as to what is 'good' or 'bad' is an ethical question, and ethical questions can only be properly considered once you have got clear about the desire that is at stake. And that question, the question of desire —'What is it?'— is the question that psychoanalysis seeks to answer. So psychoanalysis is a special tool that allows one to make ethical judgements. Here is an illustration:

It is now widely thought that much past and present legislation against homosexuals was produced by people who were themselves struggling to repress their own homosexual desires. Homophobic legislators took what they claimed was 'an ethical stance', and argued that they were 'for the good' — 'for the good heterosexuals', and 'against the bad homosexuals'.

If these people had been psychoanalysed, some might have come to see that 'ethical issues' were not foremost for them, but that they were instead trying, above all, to mislead themselves about their own desire, about their own repressed homosexuality; there is little doubt that many homophobes are fighting above all against recognition of their own homosexuality.

When you are psychoanalysed you do not come to see the world 'for what it is', without error, as the ego psychologists claim, but you can speak your own desire more clearly, and act on it. Psychoanalysis is a technique and theory for clarifying and purifying desire. Once you can identify your desire, you can make ethical assessments. But prior to knowing your desire you necessarily act in ignorance, unable to make informed ethical judgements. So psychoanalysis can allow a knowledge of desire that then facilitates the judgment 'good' or 'bad'.

For if one has to do things for the good...one is always faced with the question: for the good of whom? From that point on, things are no longer obvious. Doing things in the name of the good, and even more, in the name of the good of the other, is something that is far from protecting us...from guilt but also from all kinds of inner catastrophes.

Does psychoanalysis reduce suffering?

Sometimes. Psychoanalysis does not claim that 'when you discover your desire, all your suffering will cease and you will become happy'. The function of psychoanalysis, according to Freud was to:

convert neurotic misery to ordinary unhappiness.

Psychoanalysis, unlike religion, does not offer salvation. Indeed, Lacan thought that when people recognise and act on their desire, their life is often difficult and conflict-ridden, but in quite a different way. The new way is accepted by the subject as the price to pay, so that their suffering can take a different form:

...access to desire necessitates crossing not only all fear, but all pity, and especially not before 'The Good of The Other'... All this is experienced in the unfolding of the story so that the subject learns a little more about the deepest level of himself than he knew before... For him who goes to the end of his desire, all is not a bed of roses.

...the original distinction of psychoanalysis lay in...restoring to symptoms their meaning, according a place to the desire they mask...

Following your desire is not easy. There is often a high cost, as we saw in the case of the alcoholic man who was married, and then discovered that he was homosexual. It is the fear of paying a high cost that often insists on desires being kept unconscious and safely hidden. Psychoanalysis can sometimes reduce suffering, but only at the price of the subject giving up some enjoyment, some of the jouissance of their symptoms. So it is not unusual for someone to complete an analysis, and then to decide to keep their symptoms!

154

One man had been going to the same bar for a few years. One evening he urinated against the bar. And the next day he did the same. Because the barman had got to know him well he made the suggestion that he consult a psychoanalyst. So the unfortunate man underwent a lengthy and expensive analysis, and some years later returned to the bar, said 'Hello' to the barman, and urinated against the bar. The barman was astonished 'I don't understand; you've been psychoanalysed, but you're still peeing on my bar?' 'Yes' he said, 'I've been analysed, now I know why I do it.'

Psychoanalysis has no behavioural goals, so it is not a 'cure' for difficult or antisocial people. It does not aim to make you nicer, more successful, less inhibited, or 'better adjusted to reality'.

While psychoanalysis is uniquely privileged in working with desire, it is not the only source of information on this question. It is possible to learn something about your desire through everyday life, gardening, love affairs, or zen meditation...

...although it almost certainly won't be as efficient or as thorough.

The psychoanalyst does not transmit a body of knowledge.

But psychoanalysis is not something that can be taught like any other form of knowledge. You can study medicine to be a doctor, or mechanics to become a mechanic but to be a psychoanalyst you must — yourself— be analyzed.

Psychoanalysis is a special technique for finding your essence, the lack, division and desire that has made you live your life in the way that you do. What you actually do with this fundamental truth about yourself is not a psychoanalytic issue. Psychoanalysis has no prescriptive rules or political schemes. It does not tell you what to do, but offers a unique appreciation of what it has meant for you to be that subject.

But there are some who have had terrible lives and much suffering, who cannot work or love, for whom psychoanalysis has allowed revolutionary and dramatic changes in their lives, almost miracles.

WHAT DOES PSYCHOANALYSIS HAVE TO SAY ABOUT THE MEANING OF LIFE?

In psychoanalysis there is an answer to this question that is neither grandiose nor trivial: 'meaning' is understood as a function of language, the property of words, as the passage and rewriting of the signifier. So the meaning of life is the life of meaning. Psychoanalysis aims for an understanding of the meaning of a subject's life, through a study of his signifiers. At the end of analysis a subject can speak clearly about the meaning of his life and is then free to follow his desire, if he has the courage.

REVIEW

Is it possible to properly assess Lacan's ideas? In brief, no. Much of his large volume of esoteric work has yet to be published. And no one has yet claimed to understand all of Lacan's later topological work. Many questions and problems remain. Here are some of them:

 Is psychoanalysis a science?

What contribution can physiology, psychology, genetics and immunology make to psychoanalysis? Lacan was skeptical about the value of these disciplines for psychoanalysis.

 What contribution can psychoanalysis make outside the clinic, to other disciplines such as physics, logic, mathematics and genetics, as well as to the arts and humanities? Is psychoanalysis a good way of studying politics, mathematics, economics and anthropology?

 What is the status of the image in Lacan's later work? There is a critique of Lacan's view of the image, which does not seem to fit with his theory of signifiers. Some thinkers argue that images ought to belong —not in their own special category— but within the category of symbols, so that all images would be a kind of symbol or signifier.

But it is also too soon to properly assess Freud's work; it is only since Lacan's reinterpretation of Freud that we have started to reread and understand some of the formal theories in Freud's writing. Lacan's innovations and theories have been a massive advance in clinical and academic psychoanalysis and have already had an enormous influence on a very wide range of topics. Because of the richness and diversity of Lacan's work it is far too soon to be able to properly review his contribution to our understanding of fields that include anthropology, politics, film theory, literary criticism, history, mathematics, logic, philosophy, art, and, of course, psychoanalysis. But it is certain that Lacan's theoretical and clinical work has made a major contribution to our understanding of all that is human, ensuring that he is destined to be regarded as among the most creative of those who have theorised the human condition.

GLOSSARY

Bear in mind that this brief glossary is necessarily incomplete because Lacan rarely defined his terms, and his use of them changed over time.

A is for 'autre', French for 'other'. See other / object.

DEMAND for an object persists if the object of demand is supplied. So, for example, a child demanding of its motherer, might ask for milk, and on getting milk, he might ask for chocolate, and on getting chocolate, he might then ask for biscuits... The child is not seeking to possess or enjoy any particular physical object, but is seeking something that the motherer cannot or will not provide. Demand arises out of need, and is always the demand for love.

DESIRE is the essence of the subject, at the heart of his existence. His life revolves around it. Desire is a property of language. Desire is often unconscious.

The EGO distorts the truth and makes false connections by negotiating between the world and our unconscious desires. The ego is a complicated concept and includes the image the subject has of himself, especially of his body.

NEED is a set of biological or physiological requirements such as the need for food or warmth.

JOUISSANCE is French for 'coming' as in orgasm. It refers to Freud's and Lacan's theories of sexuality and our sexual enjoyment of a very wide range of activities that go beyond sexual intercourse, such as eating and having symptoms.

MECONNAISSANCE is misknowing especially used to describe the subject's beliefs about himself.

THE NAMES-OF-THE-FATHER are those parts of the symbolic father that have had their reference fixed, as proper or paternal names, such as 'England', or 'Jones'

fixed meanings: names

variable meanings: nouns, verbs...

The OTHER is another word for OBJECT. An object is any item that creates or supports subjectivity. These include the little object, which is the cause of desire and the object of desire, the big other, that is, the other of language, the Names-of-the-Father, signifiers or words, and the phallus.

The SIGNIFIER is roughly speaking, a word. For an explanation of 'The signifier represents the subject for another signifier', see Chapter Two.

The REAL is not reality but Lacan's term for everything that is in the category of 'the mutually exclusive' for the subject, and which always returns, for instance as the return of the repressed, when we find ourselves repeating the same patterns. See Chapter Three.

The PHALLUS is not 'The penis' but can be any observable object or item that demonstrates a rate of change, such as a swing with a child on it, a speedometer, a pregnant woman, or a penis. The phallus is one way of mak-

ing jouissance. Castration is not a surgical procedure but a reduction in the phallic function. Sexuality usually focuses on 'the other' — on the one with the phallus.

The SUBJECT is very roughly Lacan's word for 'person'.

The SYMBOLIC for Lacan is the realm of language, of words, letters and numbers.

The SYMBOLIC FATHER is any agency that separates the mother or motherer from the child. An example might be the mother's work.

The SYMPTOM is related to the idea of the phallus. Both the symptom and the phallus make jouissance or enjoyment, but the symptom speaks the subject's unconscious desire symbolically. Psychoanalytic symptoms can be idiosyncratic and so are unlike symptoms in medicine, which have relatively fixed meanings.

The UNCONSCIOUS or ID is a topological space where hidden desires live. Desires only have expression as symptoms, signifiers or words.

RECOMMENDED READING

Lacan's own writing is difficult to study on one's own. It might help to start by first reading Freud, which is far easier. If you can read the original German you will save yourself many unnecessary contradictions that are forced on English readers by systematic mistranslations. A good place to start is Freud's 'Introductory Lectures to Psychoanalysis' in the Pelican Freud Library, not the New Introductory Lectures. Having read some Freud, try some early Lacan, such as Book I and Book II of his Seminars, edited by Jacques-Alain Miller, and translated by Forrester, Cambridge University Press, 1988. Good companions at this time would be Bruce Fink's 'The Lacanian Subject' published by Princeton, 1995, Seminars 1 and 2, ed Fink et al, published by SUNY, 1995 and Dylan Evan's 'An Introductory Dictionary of Lacanian Psychoanalysis', Routledge (1996).

Do not start off with Lacan's 'Four Fundamental Concepts of Psychoanalysis' unless you are very determined; this difficult work was produced towards the end of his career.

This bibliography generally follows the material in the chapters of this book:

CHAPTER ONE

The Image and the Imaginary
See 'The Topic of the Imaginary' in: 'The Seminar of Jacques Lacan', Book I, edited Jacques-Alain Miller, translated Forrester, Cambridge University Press, 1988.

'The Mirror Stage As Formative of the Function of the I as Revealed in Psychoanalytic Experience', and 'Aggressivity in Psychoanalysis', by Lacan in 'Ecrits', translated Sheridan, Tavistock/Routledge 1977.

Socrates
'The Last Days of Socrates', Plato, Penguin Classics, is sometimes slow, but often riveting.

Ego Psychology
Hartmann, H. 'Psychoanalysis, Scientific Method and Philosophy', in 'Psychoanalysis, Scientific Method and Philosophy, a Symposium' edited by Hook, S. 1959. Almost any popular American book on 'therapy' has large doses of Ego Psychology in it.

CHAPTER TWO

Freud's 'Psychopathology of Everyday Life', is easy to read, and almost a laugh a page. It illustrates his theory of slips of the tongue and bungled actions.

The symbolic is a very general theme developed by Lacan from the 1950's onwards. One of Lacan's more accessible texts can be found in the section 'Speech in the Transference' in 'The Seminar of Jacques Lacan', Book I, edited Jacques-Alain Miller, translated Forrester, Cambridge University Press, 1988.

The ways of God cannot be understood

'The Function and Field of Speech and Language in Psychoanalysis', and 'The Agency of the Letter or Reason since Freud', are both difficult, and are in 'Ecrits', translated Sheridan, Tavistock/Routledge 1977.

CHAPTER THREE

'The real' is an idea developed throughout Lacan's later work. Freud's theory of trauma can be found in his 'Introductory Lectures to Psychoanalysis', under 'Fixation to Traumas', Pelican Freud Library Number 1.

Mathematics has become the main arena in which 'the real' —in Lacan's sense— is being formalised. See for instance the very readable: 'Mathematics, The Loss of Certainty' by Morris Kline, New York, Oxford University Press, 1980.

CHAPTER FOUR

Freud occasionally confuses the penis with the phallus. His account of the phallus, can be found in an essay mistranslated as 'On Transformations of Instinct as Exemplified in Anal Eroticism': it should be called 'On Transformations of **Drive** as Exemplified in Anal Eroticism', and is to be found in 'On Sexuality', Pelican Freud Library Number 7. Lacan's difficult theory of the phallus is in 'The Signification of the Phallus' in 'Ecrits', translated Sheridan, Tavistock/Routledge 1977.

Applications of Lacan's ideas to ideology can be found in 'The Sublime Object of Ideology', by Slavoj Zizek, Verso, 1993.

CHAPTER FIVE

Jouissance, the symptom, fantasy and the object or cause of desire are discussed throughout Lacan's later work. A difficult text on this theme is the chapter 'The Paradoxes of Jouissance' in 'The Ethics of Psychoanalysis, The Seminar of Jacques Lacan', edited Jacques-Alain Miller, translated Porter, Routledge, 1992.

CHAPTER SIX

For a clear introduction to discourse see Paul Verhaeghe's article 'From Impossibility to Inability: Lacan's Theory of the Four Discourses', in an excellent journal called 'The Letter', Spring, 1995. See also Verhaeghe's 'Does The Woman Exist?' by Rebus Press, London, 1996. Both of these are available from the specialist psychoanalysis bookseller 'Rathbone Books', 76 Haverstock Hill, London, NW3 2BD, telephone 0171 267 2848. Internet sales at Rathbook.demon.co.uk.

CHAPTER SEVEN

A good place to start on this subject, is Freud's 'On Psychopathology', Pelican Freud Library Number 10. Freud's famous obsessional case of 'The Ratman' can be found in Case Histories II, Volume 9 of the Pelican Freud Library. Freud's hysterics are in Pelican Freud Library Number 1.

CHAPTER EIGHT

See Freud's 'On Psychopathology', Pelican Freud Library Number 10, and Freud's detailed analysis of a psychotic 'Schreber', is Number 9. Lacan's seminar 'Psychosis' has been translated, and published by Routledge. Lacan's 'Introduction to the Names-of-the-Father Seminar' was published in 'October', 1987 by MIT.

If you are interested in Gödel's mathematical and logical work have a look at 'The Infinite' by A W Moore, 1990, Routledge. It is a very clear and detailed book, made easy for the beginner. If you are brave or have a knowledge of logic or maths you might try 'The Work of Kurt Gödel' in 'Gödel's Theorem in Focus', edited by Shanker, published by Croom Helm, 1988, pages 48-60.

CHAPTER NINE

Feminine Sexuality
This is a difficult topic. Freud's papers are a good place to start: 'On the Universal Tendency to Debasement in the Sphere of Love', 'The Dissolution of the Oedipus Complex' and 'Some Psychical Consequences of the Anatomical Sex Distinction' in 'On Sexuality', Pelican Freud Library Number 7.

'Does The Woman Exist? From Freud's hysteric to Lacan's feminine' is a fine book by Paul Verhaeghe, translated by Marc du Ry, published by Rebus Press, 1996.

See parts of Lacan's seminar 'En Corp / Encore' in 'Feminine Sexuality, especially 'Feminine Sexuality in Psychoanalytic Doctrine' and 'God and the Jouissance of the Woman', Jacques Lacan and The Ecole Freudienne', translated by Rose, edited by Mitchel and Rose, 1982, Macmillian.

If you are interested in Cantor's mathematical work, consider 'The Infinite' by A W Moore, 1990, Routledge. It is a very clear and detailed book, made easy for the beginner. 'Georg Cantor, His Mathematics and Philosophy of the Infinite', by Joseph Dauben, Princeton, 1990, is interesting but difficult and includes some higher mathematics.

CHAPTER TEN

Lacan's most famous work on time is "Logical Time and the Assertion of Anticipated Certainty", but he later changed his mind! This article is translated in 'The Newsletter of the Freudian Field', 1988, Volume 2, Number 2. Lacan's latest and least comprehensible work was on topology.

CHAPTER ELEVEN

'The Ethics of Psychoanalysis, The Seminar of Jacques Lacan', edited Jacques-Alain Miller, translated Porter, Routledge, 1992, is a very rich and dense text. Challenging and stimulating, but not for the beginner.

Also consider:

- Death and Desire, Psychoanalytic Theory in Lacan's Return to Freud, Richard Boothby, Routledge, 1991.

- Returning to Freud, Clinical Psychoanalysis in the School of Lacan, ed Schneiderman, Yale University Press, 1980. This book demonstrates how Lacanian ideas are used in practice with clients.

- A short and clear paper on a clinical approach informed by Lacanian theory can be found in a short paper called 'Reflection on Impasse' by James Gorney, in 'Criticism and Lacan, Essays and Dialogue on Language, Structure, and the Unconscious', edited by Patrick Hogan and Lalita Pandit, published by The University of Georgia Press, 1990.

- An excellent book is 'An Introductory Dictionary of Lacanian Psychoanalysis', by Dylan Evans, Routledge (1996). This explains clearly many of Lacan's technical terms, how he came to change them during his career, and his influences.

There are curently two organisations in England that are seriously interested in working clinically with Lacan's ideas:

The Centre for Freudian Analysis and Research
76 Haverstock Hill,
London, NW3

phone number: 0171 639 8289

The London Circle of The European School of Psychoanalysis
48 Bonnington Square
London
SW8 1TQ

phone number: 0171 628 3380

ACADEMIC WORK

There is a growth at the moment of psychoanalytic courses offered at UK universities, for many the focus is on Lacan's work. For a list contact the Higher Education Network for Research and Information in Psychoanalysis (THERIP):

Dr E Reid
THERIP
St Michaels
South Mimms
Herts
EN6 3PA

Language and its structures exist prior to the moment at which each subject at a certain point in his mental development makes his entry into it

165

What mystics have in common with women is a special relationship to the infinite

The ways of God cannot be understood

It must be remarked that the lateness of dentition and of walking, a lateness correlative for the majority of bodily equipment and functions, indicates in the infant a total vital impotence which lasts through the first two years. We must not hesitate to recognise man as an animal prematurely born

HOW TO GET GREAT THINKERS TO COME TO YOUR HOME...

To order any current titles of Writers and Readers *For Beginners*™ books, please fill out the coupon below and enclose a check made out to **Writers and Readers Publishing, Inc.** To order by phone (with Master Card or Visa), or to receive a <u>free catalog</u> of all our *For Beginners*™ books, please call (212) 982-3158.

Price per book: $11.00

Individual Order Form (clip out or copy complete page)

Book Title	Quantity	Amount
	Sub Total:	
N.Y. residents add 8 1/4% sales tax		
Shipping & Handling ($3.00 for the first book; $.60 for each additional book)		
	TOTAL	

Name _____

Address _____

City _____ State _____ Zip Code _____

Phone number (___)_____

MC / VISA (circle one) Account # _____ Expires _____

Send check or money order to: **Writers and Readers Publishing**, P.O. Box 461 Village Station, New York, NY 10014 (212) 982-3158, fx (212) 777-4924; In the U.K: **Airlift Book Company**, 8, The Arena, Mollison Ave., Enfield, EN3 7NJ, England 0181.804.0044. Or contact us for a <u>FREE</u> <u>CATALOG</u> of all our *For Beginners*™ titles.

Writers and Readers

Addiction & Recovery ($11.00)
African History ($9.95)
Arabs & Israel ($12.00)
Architecture ($11.00)
Babies ($9.95)
Biology ($11.00)
Black History ($9.95)
Black Holocaust ($11.00)
Black Panthers ($11.00)
Black Women ($9.95)
Brecht ($9.95)
Buddha ($11.00)
Chomsky ($11.00)
Classical Music ($9.95)
Computers ($11.00)
Derrida ($11.00)
DNA ($9.95)
Domestic Violence ($11.00)
Elvis ($6.95)
Erotica ($7.95)
Food ($7.95)
Foucault ($9.95)
Freud ($9.95)
Health Care ($9.95)
Heidegger ($9.95)
Hemingway ($9.95)
History of Clowns ($11.00)
I-Ching ($11.00)
Ireland ($9.95)
Islam ($9.95)
Jazz ($11.00)
Jewish Holocaust ($11.00)
J.F.K. ($9.95)
Judaism ($11.00)
Jung ($11.00)
Kierkegaard ($11.00)
Lacan ($11.00)
Malcolm X ($9.95)
Mao ($9.95)
Martial Arts ($11.00)
Miles Davis ($9.00)
Nietzsche ($11.00)
Opera ($11.00)
Orwell ($4.95)
Pan-Africanism ($9.95)
Philosophy ($11.00)
Plato ($11.00)
Psychiatry ($9.95)
Rainforests ($7.95)
Sartre ($11.00)
Saussure ($11.00)
Sex ($9.95)
Shakespeare ($11.00)
Structuralism ($11.00)
UNICEF ($11.00)
United Nations ($11.00)
World War II ($8.95)
Zen ($11.00)